WOODLAND WALKS
in South-East England

Webb&Bower
O|S Ordnance Survey

WOODLAND WALKS
in South-East England
Gerald Wilkinson

First published in Great Britain in 1986 by
Webb & Bower (Publishers) Limited,
9 Colleton Crescent, Exeter, Devon EX2 4BY, and
Ordnance Survey,
Romsey Road, Maybush, Southampton So9 4 DH
in association with
Michael Joseph Limited,
27 Wright's Lane, London W8 5SL

Designed by Peter Wrigley

Production by Nick Facer

British Library Cataloguing in Publication Data

Wilkinson, Gerald
    The Ordnance Survey woodland walks in
    South-East England.
    1. Forests and forestry—England—South East
    2. South-East (England)—Description and travel
    —Guide-books
    I. Title
    914.22′04858   DA670.S63

    ISBN 0–86350–056–0

Typeset in Great Britain by Keyspools Limited, Golborne, Lancashire
Printed and bound in Great Britain by Hazell Watson and Viney Limited,
Member of the BPCC Group, Aylesbury, Bucks

TITLE PAGE
In the Ashdown Forest, looking towards Sevenoaks

Contents

Introduction

Accessible woods, or 'access woodlands' as they are called by Essex County Council, are not in short supply in south-east England. This fact should be celebrated, for we hear a great deal about the destruction of native woods and perhaps forget to look at those we have, quite close at hand. To my surprise, I found myself spending a great deal of time in Surrey, Kent and south Essex – areas I had previously despised as suburban. After a few over-confident false starts, when I learnt that in this part of the country one must pick one's way carefully, Surrey particularly was an eye-opener.

Nearly 29,000 acres of Surrey are common land and, apart from some Ministry of Defence preserves, accessible to everyone to walk where they will. Much of this common land is wooded, and about 4000 acres are actually managed as woodland by local authorities, private owners and the National Trust. This is important, because properly managed woodland is a great deal more interesting than neglected wilderness (though that has its place). Altogether 35,000 acres of countryside in Surrey are open to the public: nearly one-twelfth of the total area. This compares with something like one-hundredth for England and Wales, though of course many upland areas in addition are taken to be 'open countryside' while legally they are private land. Commons owned by urban district councils and by the National Trust have to open to the public, but this accounts for only a fifth of the commons in England and Wales (Scotland is assumed to have no commons).

Kent also has well-wooded commons close to central London, and, further out, fine ancient woodlands and notable forests. On the Hertfordshire and Essex boundaries of Greater London, not only does Epping Forest penetrate deep into the urban area, but the county councils also have set up a string of country parks and the above-mentioned 'access woodlands'. Country parks vary: some are only elaborate sports centres, while others are pieces of serious working countryside designed to be accessible and remaining beautiful. The wooded country parks of Essex and the important Great Wood Country Park in Hertfordshire belong in the latter class. To the north-west, the Chilterns are well known for beechwood walks and interesting scrubland. Middlesex, before it disappeared, was rather less fortunate, but there are wooded commons about Ruislip.

London itself is often remarked on as full of trees and parks, and there is woodland too; probably much more, in small pockets, than I have been able to identify. If you live in London, a large-scale map of your area (about six inches to the mile, 1:10000) may be much better value than a tube ticket. I didn't even explore Greenwich Park or Hampton Court, and I forgot that Surbiton has a nature reserve called The Wood. Even a stroll in Hyde Park and Kensington Gardens can teach one something about trees, for more than two hundred different species and varieties are planted there.

Of course, when you think about it, it is not surprising that the greatest concentration of people has the best collection of woodlands. Woods had to be maintained near London for fuel. The railways brought coal to the fireside and soon took city workers to country residences, so that when coppices for firewood became redundant they found a public with a vested interest in preserving their woodland character. The coppices still also supplied many of the essentials of life well into the twentieth century: fencing, chairs, tool handles, rakes and brooms, barrels and baskets, rolling pins, toys, billiard cues, wheel-spokes, walking sticks, wattles, bark for tanning leather, fine charcoal for the gunpowder used in slow-burning fuses. Only recently have we acquired the habit, along with worse sorts of madness, of assembling consumer goods from bits of unsuitable, non-renewable material and transporting them over vast distances. There were broom squires ('squarers') working on

Hindhead Common, still in 1918. But the Hindhead Preservation Society had already acquired the land some years before.

Octavia's Wood, a silent, simple beechwood not twenty miles from Charing Cross, is named after Octavia Hill, one of the founders of the National Trust in 1895. But other beechwoods, near High Wycombe, still heard the crack of the chair bodger's froe and the regular song of the pole lathe, until the late 1940s.

To speak of preserving a wood is to imply woodland management along traditional lines, for woods are not monuments. Providing access, lavatories, information centres, managing 'by the book' rather than from need, keeping alive outdated crafts; all in their ways degrade the character of the surviving native woods. But at the least we gain an insight into ways of life forgotten for some generations, even for centuries. We begin to understand that woodland is a crucially important part of the intricate web of our country's ecology – a web that nowadays holds together very precariously. At the best, we discover natural creatures and natural patterns that we never expected to be privileged to see. And, in the nature of woods, we can always slip away and keep our own counsel.

Besides those interesting coppices, some, of chestnut, still producing posts and palings, others of lime, hazel, oak, hornbeam or ash, at least playing their parts in various conservation schemes, there is an enormous range of woodland in the south-east. Ancient forest and parkland oaks can be seen in quantity at Windsor and Richmond, Alice Holt, Hatfield House, Knole Park; oaks and hornbeams at Thorndon Park in Essex, and large hornbeams at Hatfield Forest, near Bishop's Stortford. High beechwoods can be found near the sea on the North and South Downs, and, quieter, inland in Kent and Surrey; best known of all are the beechwoods of Ashridge in Hertfordshire. The Chilterns carry open beechwoods through Buckinghamshire (touching Oxfordshire) and into Berkshire where the Ridge Way creeps out westwards. Epping Forest, with pollard beech and hornbeam, is a wood-pasture now unused and growing to high forest, not less elegant for that.

There are older pollard beeches at Burnham and, less well known, in Brantridge Forest.

There is a famous yew wood at Kingley Vale in Sussex, and a smaller, even darker one at Boxley, Kent. Yews, finely shaped but not quite woodland, cluster on the common above Watlington in Oxfordshire. Boxwoods, more or less wild, survive in Arundel Park and at Great Kimble in Oxfordshire as well as at Box Hill – and nowhere else in the country so far as I know.

The typical English wood of oak standards, widely spaced and with hard understorey, usually coppiced, is now hard to find in the south-east, though not unknown. The foresters always had their eye on those useless acres of hazel coppice. H. L. Edlin, in 1956, indicated a surplus of 140,000 acres in the country as a whole. Hornbeam coppice has more often been preserved, perhaps because it is so distinctive. Small-leaved lime, sometimes quoted as the dominant tree of the Midlands about 5000 years ago, can be seen in quite a number of woodland reserves, notably at Chalkney Wood in the Colne Valley. Occasional groups of aspen are to be found in Essex woods.

The only birch coppice I know in the south-east is in Epping Forest, unless you count Wimbledon Common, but birch occurs everywhere and is elegant on the sandy heaths of Ashdown Forest as in the heathy commons of the Bagshot Sands. These sandy soils in prehistoric time supported pine forests which were entirely removed under human occupation. The Scots pine was reintroduced, usually from European stock, and is now naturalized, spreading once again. Such are the complexities of the woodland story.

Elms are now rare. Wych elm, the oldest of the several native species, proved to be most resistant to the disease, and it is still an element of eastern woods, with some of its hybrids. Whitebeam is common in all the chalklands, usually at beechwood margins, and the wild cherry is said to be on the increase. It is the only broadleaved tree that can compete in high beechwood. Wild service, well known and often described as an indicator of ancient woodland, turned up where expected and hardly ever anywhere else. Maple is a good hedge tree and uncommon in woodland even where it is expected. A giant specimen, 77 feet high, at Mote Park, Maidstone, is all the more surprising. Of introduced alien broadleaves, the sycamore is not the pernicious weed of the forest that it threatens to be in the west of the country, but this is not for lack of seedlings, as gardeners will know. Horse-chestnut keeps to its suburban status and is rarely naturalized. Norway maple, planted as a forestry tree in one wood near Sevenoaks, is frequently planted elsewhere by the Forestry Commission as an 'amenity tree'. (Amenity means 'pleasant feature'.) It is naturalized only locally. *Robinia pseudoacacia*, the false acacia or locust tree, was an enthusiasm of William Cobbett, but is rarely seen except as a park, garden or street tree. It is naturalized on the top of Hampstead Hill and there is a very old specimen at Hatfield House.

Ancient woods are full of thriving natives, the balance altered over the centuries, but still the same species that naturally grew there before man appeared. This leaves little space for aliens. But elm incursions now leave gaps.

The main forestry tree of the south-east is the Corsican pine, and the Scots pine is used a good deal. You will come across little more than a handful of alien conifers in the Forestry Commission plantations: Norway spruce, Sitka spruce, Serbian spruce; western red cedar and western hemlock; giant fir and noble fir, and larch, usually the hybrid between the European and the Japanese. All of these and many other conifers and broadleaves of timber potential (including the southern beeches) can be seen and studied in the forest plots of Bedgebury Pinetum. Here you can learn the trees by touch and smell as well as by sight. The pinetum also offers walks along vistas, unrivalled in Britain, of the most beautiful specimen trees and groups.

Sheffield Park and Wakehurst Place in Sussex are great arboreta with no counterparts north of the Thames, though Woburn Park pinetum was one of the earliest and finest. Wisley and Kew are of course world famous. Other arboreta and collections of trees are at:

Hants	Itchen Abbas, Avington House
Kent	Scotney Castle, Lamberhurst (NT), Sandling Park, Hythe, Dunorlan Park in Tunbridge Wells
London	Regent's Park, Osterley Park, Syon House, Chiswick House, Marble Hill, Twickenham, Forty Hall, Enfield
Suffolk	Abbey Gardens, Bury St Edmunds
Surrey	Claremont, Esher (NT), Winkworth Arboretum (NT) near Godalming
Sussex	Nymans, Handcross (NT), West Dean Arboretum, Tilgate Park, Crawley

Key

The book is divided into sections which follow on numerically from west to east and south to north of the region. At the beginning of each section the relevant Ordnance Survey Landranger sheet numbers are listed. Each entry is headed with factual information in the form below:

a   b   c

Burrator Forest *568 694*, ♀ ✿, *1000 acres, paths and a forest road, WA*

d   e

a Ordnance Survey National Grid reference – usually of the nearest car park
b Type of woodland: ♀ deciduous
     ♠ coniferous ✿ marsh
c Size of wooded area
d Type of walk
e Owner of site

How to find a grid reference

The refence for Burrator Forest is *568 694*

56 – Can be found in the top and bottom margins of the relevant map sheet (identified at the start of each book section). It is the reference number for one of the grid lines running north/south on the map.
69 – Can be found in the left and right hand margins of the relevant map sheet. It is the reference number for one of the grid lines running east/west on the map.

These numbers locate the bottom left hand corner of the kilometre grid square in which the car park for Burrator Forest appears. The remaining figures of the reference (*568 694*) pinpoint the feature within the grid square to the nearest 100 metres as shown in the diagram below.

The following abbreviations are used:

AONB	Area of outstanding natural beauty
CNT	*County Naturalists' Trust*
CP	Country Park
FC	Forestry Commission
FNR	Forest Nature Reserve
fp	footpath
GLC	Greater London Council
LA	Local Authority
LNR	Local Nature Reserve
MAFF	Ministry of Agriculture Fisheries and Food
NC	Nature Conservancy
NNR	National Nature Reserve
NT	National Trust
NTS	National Trust for Scotland
pf	private forestry
SSSI	Site of Special Scientific Interest
SWT	Scottish Wildlife Trust
WA	Water Authority
WT	Woodland Trust

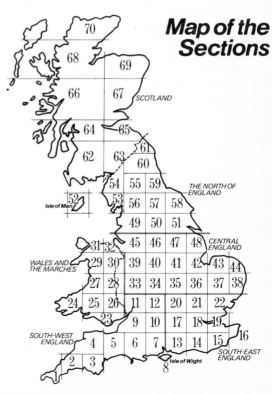

Map of the Sections

SCOTLAND

THE NORTH OF ENGLAND

CENTRAL ENGLAND

WALES AND THE MARCHES

Isle of Man

SOUTH-WEST ENGLAND

SOUTH-EAST ENGLAND

Isle of Wight

56   57

70 ——————————————— 70

Burrator Forest Parking → ✕

69 ——————————————— 69

56   **Grid reference** *5669*   57

The dotted lines within the square do not appear on the face of the map

1:316,800 maps

RELIEF

Feet	Metres	
		· 274
		Heights in feet above mean sea level
3000	914	
2000	610	
1400	427	
1000	305	Contours at 200ft intervals
600	183	
200	61	
0	0	To convert feet to metres multiply by 0·3048

TOURIST INFORMATION

- Abbey, Cathedral, Priory
- Ancient monument
- Aquarium
- Camp site
- Caravan site
- Castle
- Cave
- Country park
- Craft centre
- Garden
- Golf course or links
- Historic house
- Information centre
- Motor racing
- Museum
- Nature or forest trail
- Nature reserve
- Other tourist feature
- Picnic site
- Preserved railway
- Racecourse
- Skiing
- Viewpoint
- Wildlife park
- Youth hostel
- Zoo

ROADS Not necessarily rights of way

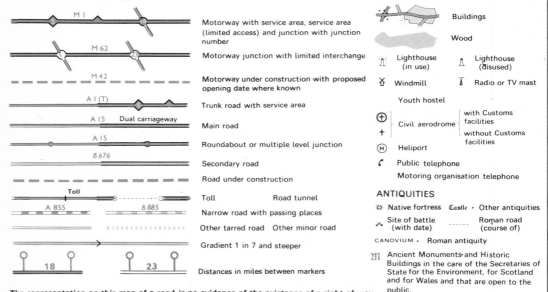

- M 1 — Motorway with service area, service area (limited access) and junction with junction number
- M 62 — Motorway junction with limited interchange
- M 42 — Motorway under construction with proposed opening date where known
- A 1 (T) — Trunk road with service area
- A 15 Dual carriageway — Main road
- A 15 — Roundabout or multiple level junction
- B 676 — Secondary road
- Road under construction
- Toll — Toll   Road tunnel
- A 855   B 885 — Narrow road with passing places
- Other tarred road   Other minor road
- Gradient 1 in 7 and steeper
- 18   23 — Distances in miles between markers

The representation on this map of a road is no evidence of the existence of a right of way

GENERAL FEATURES

- Buildings
- Wood
- Lighthouse (in use)
- Lighthouse (disused)
- Windmill
- Radio or TV mast
- Youth hostel
- Civil aerodrome { with Customs facilities / without Customs facilities }
- Heliport
- Public telephone
- Motoring organisation telephone

ANTIQUITIES

- ✳ Native fortress   𝕮𝖆𝖘𝖙𝖑𝖊 · Other antiquities
- Site of battle (with date)
- Roman road (course of)
- CANOVIUM · Roman antiquity
- 𝔪 Ancient Monuments and Historic Buildings in the care of the Secretaries of State for the Environment, for Scotland and for Wales and that are open to the public.

WATER FEATURES

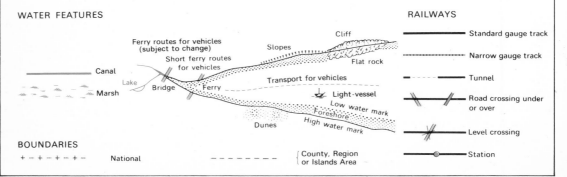

- Canal
- Marsh
- Lake
- Bridge
- Ferry
- Ferry routes for vehicles (subject to change)
- Short ferry routes for vehicles
- Transport for vehicles
- Slopes
- Cliff
- Flat rock
- Light-vessel
- Low water mark
- Foreshore
- High water mark
- Dunes

RAILWAYS

- Standard gauge track
- Narrow gauge track
- Tunnel
- Road crossing under or over
- Level crossing
- Station

BOUNDARIES

- + — + — + — + — National
- — — — — — — { County, Region or Islands Area

1:50,000 maps

ROADS AND PATHS Not necessarily rights of way

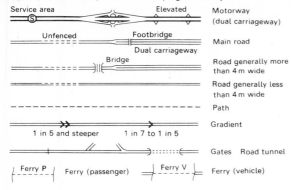

Service area ⓢ Elevated	Motorway (dual carriageway)
Unfenced Dual carriageway	Main road
Bridge	Road generally more than 4 m wide
	Road generally less than 4 m wide
	Path
1 in 5 and steeper 1 in 7 to 1 in 5	Gradient
	Gates Road tunnel
Ferry P Ferry (passenger) Ferry V	Ferry (vehicle)

PUBLIC RIGHTS OF WAY (Not applicable to Scotland)

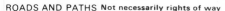

Public rights of way indicated by these symbols have been
derived from Definitive Maps as amended by later enactments
or instruments held by Ordnance Survey on and are shown subject
to the limitations imposed by the scale of mapping

**The representation on this map of any other road, track or
path is no evidence of the existence of a right of way**

TOURIST INFORMATION

ℹ Information centre	☎ Telephone, public/motoring organisation
🅿 Parking	⛳ Golf course or links
P	PC Public convenience (in rural areas)
✗ Picnic site	☀ Viewpoint

GENERAL FEATURES

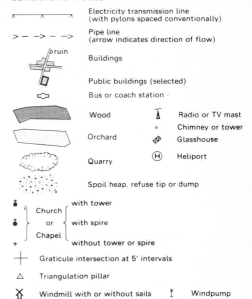

	Electricity transmission line (with pylons spaced conventionally)
> - -> - ->	Pipe line (arrow indicates direction of flow)
ruin	Buildings
	Public buildings (selected)
	Bus or coach station -
	Wood
	Orchard
	Quarry
	Spoil heap, refuse tip or dump

		Radio or TV mast	
		Chimney or tower	
		Glasshouse	
Ⓗ		Heliport	

Church or Chapel — with tower / with spire / without tower or spire

+ Graticule intersection at 5' intervals

△ Triangulation pillar

✗ Windmill with or without sails   Windpump

HEIGHTS

•144   Heights are to the nearest
metre above mean sea level

Heights shown close to a triangulation pillar refer to the station
height at ground level and not necessarily to the summit.

WATER FEATURES

Marsh or salting, Cliff, Slopes, High water mark, Low water mark, Towpath Lock, Flat rock, Lighthouse (in use), Aqueduct, Canal, Ford, Sand, Dunes, Beacon, Weir, Bridge, Normal tidal limit, Lighthouse (disused), Shingle, Lake, Footbridge, Mud

======= Canal (dry)

ABBREVIATIONS

P	Post office
PH	Public house
MS	Milestone
MP	Milepost
CH	Clubhouse
PC	Public convenience (in rural areas)
TH	Town Hall, Guildhall or equivalent
CG	Coastguard

BOUNDARIES

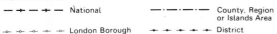

— + — + — National	—·—·—·— County, Region or Islands Area
—·—○—·— London Borough	— + — + — District

ANTIQUITIES

VILLA Roman   ⚔ Battlefield (with date)   + Position of antiquity which cannot be drawn to scale

Castle Non-Roman   ⁂ Tumulus

The revision date of archaeological information varies over the sheet

RAILWAYS

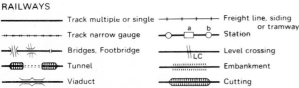

Track multiple or single	Freight line, siding or tramway
Track narrow gauge	Station
Bridges, Footbridge	Level crossing
Tunnel	Embankment
Viaduct	Cutting

HOW TO GIVE A GRID REFERENCE (BRITISH NATIONAL GRID)

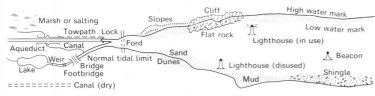

100 000 Metre GRID SQUARE IDENTIFICATION	TO GIVE A GRID REFERENCE TO NEAREST 100 METRES
SN / SO 200 / SS / ST / 300	**SAMPLE POINT: The Talbots**
	1. Read letters identifying 100 000 metre square in which the point lies. ST
	2. FIRST QUOTE EASTINGS Locate first VERTICAL grid line to LEFT of point and read LARGE figures labelling the line either in the top or bottom margin or on the line itself. Estimate tenths from grid line to point. 05 7
	3. AND THEN QUOTE NORTHINGS Locate first HORIZONTAL grid line BELOW point and read LARGE figures labelling the line either in the left or right margin or on the line itself. Estimate tenths from grid line to point. 70 7
IGNORE the SMALLER figures of any grid number: these are for finding the full coordinates. Use ONLY the LARGER figure of the grid number.	**SAMPLE REFERENCE** ST 057 707
EXAMPLE: ²69 000m	For local referencing grid letters may be omitted.

SCALE 1:316 800 or 5 MILES to 1 INCH

0 1 km = 0·6214 mile 5 .... 10 ...... Kilometres 15

0 1 mile = 1·61 kms .... 5 ...... Miles 10

SOUTH DOWNS WOODLANDS

Queen Elizabeth Forest Park *718 185,*
♀ ♠, 1400 acres, various walks and trails
based on 6 picnic places, FC CC jointly
Some of the trails have WCs and provision for
the disabled. Features include School Trail,
Craft Trail, Wayfaring Course, Pony Trekking
Trails, Ancient Farm; Park Centre with
bookstall and slide theatre, exhibition and
cafeteria. There is a charge for parking.

The park also contains **Butser Hill**, *713 200*,
with a high point of 888 feet, the western end
of the South Downs: a car park with some
marvellous views – not forest but grassland,
with sheep to keep it grazed. Sheep rearing
management demonstrations are held near the
Park Centre. The centre is the only way in for
cars and has a special link road and underpass
from the A3(T), 3 miles south of Petersfield.

Queen Elizabeth Forest is of beech, mostly
planted since 1930, with old yews and remains
of juniper scrub and thorn. This is not a typical
Forestry Commission forest – it is much more
organized than usual and it costs money – not a
lot, but you cannot get in free. The park is run
as a piece of 'working Hampshire countryside'.
At least it provides some exciting outings for
Southampton schoolchildren, and the centre
offers a valuable introduction to forest ways
aimed at a wide variety of people.

The highest and most remote parking place
in the woods, called Juniper, has a crafts
exhibition and is the start of a tree-recognition
trail – the trees are numbered to agree with a
leaflet with some extra ones which are listed on
a notice at the exhibition site. Craft examples
in the exhibition are fairly downbeat, such as
lapped fencing, ignoring the qualities of the
local timber as one of the finest hardwoods.
There is a reconstructed Victorian sawpit
(for two-handed plank sawing) but there is no
wood-turning. The Tree Trail is fine, but the

Queen Elizabeth Forest Park from Butser Hill

leaflet irritatingly condescends with bold line drawings of, for instance, beech leaves which you can see millions of on site.

On the Juniper Walk you have fine views of Butser Down between the beeches (some pine nurses remaining).

Butser Down, silent, high, inspiring, won my affections more than the woodlands: but it could be awful in August. From the Butser Trail you can look down a deep coombe, seagulls turning below as if you were on the Cliffs of Moher. Beyond are beautifully shaped wooded hills, and fields of sheep. A line of pylons spoils the view – there is always something. For some reason the radio mast with its peculiar dishes on top of Butser Hill is not offensive, though why it should be essentially different from, though obviously less boring than, electricity pylons, I cannot think.

The School Trail is good, but again the leaflet, though very informative, adopts an arch manner, with difficult words like 'tree planting' underlined. Can you list ten reasons why we need woods?

The Forest of Bere is a region inland from Portsmouth, long ago drunk up and deforested, and built upon by Waterlooville. Havant Forest, The Holt and Havant Thicket are under Forestry Commission exploitation, but there is a patch or strip of coppice oak in the Thicket area. Between Denmead and North Boarhunt (excellent forest names) are many finely shaped oaks which must be the descendants of forest trees: the dark shapes of the Ports Down beyond. The name Forest of Bere is kept by the Forestry Commission for a relatively small area of woodland including what is described as a remnant of the forest in the Meon Valley: West Walk.

West Walk *596 124, ♀ ♣, 900 acres, easy 2 hours, FC*

From the A333 turn north to Hundred Acres, 1 mile east of Wickham. The car park is the quietest of three and is called West Walk – actually it is to the south-east of the woods. The younger trees are on this side, so it is worth combining the walk, waymarked in

Winter colours in Bere Forest West Walk

green, with the Woodend Path, marked in yellow, which begins on the other side of the wood. The route then includes, besides pine and *Tsuga*, an area of relatively old forest oaks. Our path follows a stream near the Woodend car park into a beechwood, and proceeds to more open land with gorse and young larch, returning through oak, beech and holly: woodland of open and natural appearance. Then turn right and uphill on to the public footpath to a tall stand of Corsican pine close to the West Walk car park. The whole effect of this fragment of forest is happy, varied and picturesque. The style varies from familiar, straightforward conifer farming to neglected oakwood: from gravel to clay. There are beechwoods, a birchwood and a patch of open grass with a scattering of Christmas trees, and other small surprises. Bird life is fairly busy and there are rabbits and squirrels: there are said to be roe deer but I saw no sign of them. There are supposed to be over 200,000 human visitors a year: paths are certainly well worn, but there is plenty of natural regeneration of the broadleaves. I met a lady with two dogs who was looking for the lesser spotted woodpecker.

Alice Holt Forest *812 436 (Visitors' Centre), ♀ ♣, 2000 acres, trails, FC*

Alice Holt, the site of large Roman potteries, seems to have been a royal hunting preserve since Saxon times, when, we are told, bears, wolves, foxes, martens, wild cat and red deer were hunted. It was from Aelfsige, Bishop of

Winchester, that it got its name, later Axes Holte. *Holt* is Old Saxon for a wood. Much of the hunting forest, then very large since it included Woolmer Forest to the south, would be heathland, but timber was taken for Westminster Great Hall and Windsor Castle. Foresters appointed by the Crown did much as they liked, and the gentry round about poached habitually, simply paying their fines when required. By the time of Henry VIII naval dockyards on the Thames were being supplied, presumably via the River Wey, and the tradition of 'cultivating Navy timber' continued until the age of steel. From 1812, some 1600 acres were enclosed and planted with oak. By 1903 there was much surplus oak, the great, large-limbed trees being no longer required, and Alice Holt was transformed by the Commissioners for Crown Lands by the planting of larch, Douglas fir, Scots pine and Corsican pine. In 1924 the forest automatically

became the concern of the new Forestry Commission.

New plantations in the southernmost Straits Inclosure ensure that oak will dominate in that area, and many old trees are preserved elsewhere in the forest. Deer, repeatedly removed in the last two centuries as a threat to timber production, returned from about 1960 in the form of a roe deer population, now controlled at about 120 individuals. The Forestry Commission's Research Branch is located at Alice Holt, and there are fields planted with quaintly named poplar cultivars.

The turnpike from Farnham to Petersfield was built in 1826, commendably straight but, short-sightedly, through the middle of the forest. Now, as the A325, it is a hazard; though as you drive south towards the forest all the dark trees do look grand and romantic.

At Bucks Horn Oak on the A325 the Forest Centre is signposted. There are four car parks

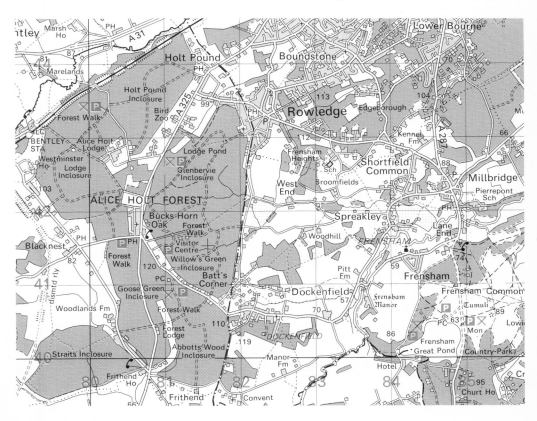

A poplar hybrid in the trial plots at Alice Holt
(*Populus nigra × trichocarpa*)

Floor of a southern beech plantation, Alice Holt

with picnic sites and forest walks, one suitable for wheelchairs.

The **Willow's Green Trail** starts from the Visitors' Centre (open from 11 am to 4 pm on weekdays and some holidays) which has leaflets and a historical display as well as hot and cold water. Continue on the forest road for Lodge Pond parking place if you just want an open place to play ball games – otherwise this is too near the main road for peace and quiet. You can fish in the pond; day permits are available from the Chief Forester.

The **Arboretum Trail**, *802 434*, provides a short, level route for wheelchairs, and a longer trail for walkers. There are good plots of the two main southern beeches, and stands or groups of other major forest trees, a collection of Lawson cultivars etc: all more instructive if the labelling were better maintained, but a very interesting and pleasant woodland walk.

Abbotts Wood, *812 410*, $\frac{1}{2}$ mile along the Dockenfield road from Bucks Horn Oak, is the 'Habitat Trail'. The leaflet mentions little unusual, but the point is made that Abbotts Wood with its varied terrain, specialized management and varied planting provides maximum diversity of habitat. Rides are cut at times which avoid destruction of food plants, old and dying trees are retained for insect life, ponds are 'rehabilitated'. A 'few hundred' wild flowers can be found here, and lists of all species, birds and insects as well, are available to those 'genuinely interested'. The car park is very quiet – scented and heavily shaded by western red cedar. The trail leads through tall Corsican pines, unbelievably only forty years old. There are oak plantations dating from 1820, 1935 and 1950, pines of 1930, red cedar of 1962, and hemlock of 1971. A pasture field provides useful edges, and rides contain many adventitious natives such as hazel and sallows. On this trail the Forestry Commission's helpful signs are not very clear as to direction, and some patience is needed.

For **Goose Green**, *804 416*, turn off the A325 opposite the Halfway House pub. This is the History Trail, including oaks planted around 1820, when deer were removed and steps taken to repair our 'wooden walls' after the Napoleonic threat. As everyone knows, but no one knew then, the ships were soon to be made of iron. There is a reconstructed Roman kiln, this having been the site of a large Roman pottery. Goose Green, and Straits Inclosure to the south, will remain predominantly oakwoods.

Woolmer Forest towards Petersfield is a mess of tidy housing, rifle ranges, air strips and the Ministry-of-Defence-only knows what else. It must be said, however, that the modern Army plays an important part in conservation, if only by imposing zero land use and restricting public access to nil, which means no gathering of wild specimens for gardens or collections. Also, I understand that in this and other areas of long occupation by the Army, more positive conservation is undertaken: I hope it does not take the misguided form of planting trees and clearing scrub.

Turn right at Whitehall in Woolmer Forest, onto the B3006 for Selborne Hill.

Selborne Hill *730 330, ♀, 257 acres, fp, NT*

Sacred to naturalists, the National Trust land includes Selborne Hanger (the beechwood on the northern slope) and the common which occupies the top of the hill. It is a chalk hill but with patches of upper greensand – and what I call mud. The common, once presumably wood-pasture, is neglected to the point of fantasy, the great, wounded, grey trunks of beeches now surrounded by thorns which droop and sway into natural arches covered by ivy. A wood to dream in, if you are not searching avidly for some native plant or creature. There are thickets outside the shading beech canopy which seem impenetrable except to the birds which are for once much in evidence. There are many rides and footpaths, so that an Ordnance Survey 1:50,000 map is poor guidance: if you try to go straight across you will probably arrive back where you started – that is one way of taking a

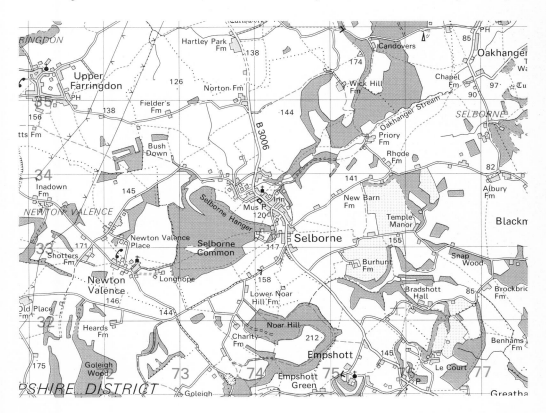

walk. In the middle is a large patch of open grassland, adding considerably to the variety of habitat, but posing a problem: why is it not overgrown like the rest of the common? In a deer park it might be described as a laund by those who feel the term lawn to be too prosaic. Perhaps it was a sort of village green for the Selborne folk, with their 'plaistow' in the narrow valley below.

The most important, and probably the oldest, path is from Newton Valence to Selborne, entering the wood at the west side near a lovely house called Longhope. This path runs roughly north-east by east (or south-west

The path to Selborne Common by Longhope House

by west) if you use a compass, and passes diagonally across the lawn I have mentioned to the east end of the Hanger slope. Another path follows the contour through the beeches of the Hanger, and you can descend opposite the church, where the yew measured in 1789 by Gilbert White as 23 feet is now 26 feet. To do

the walk in reverse, perhaps more logically, start at the lane by the museum opposite the church, and go up the hill by White's zig-zag path until you meet the transverse path.

Of Woolmer Forest Gilbert White wrote:

> The Royal Forest of Wolmer is a tract of land about seven miles in length, two and a half in breadth . . . this royalty consists entirely of sand covered with heath and fern; but is somewhat diversified with hills and dales, without having one standing tree in the whole extent. In the bottoms, where the waters stagnate, are many bogs, which formerly abounded with subterraneous trees.

Of Alice Holt he wrote:

> Ayles Holt: a strong loam, of a miry nature, carrying a good turf and abounding with oaks which grow to be large timber; while Wolmer is nothing but a hungry, sandy, barren waste. . . . Fallow deer are never seen in Wolmer, red deer never known to haunt thicket or glade of the Holt.

The A325 continues southwards; it is a road for the forests. Beyond Woolmer Forest turn left at Liss on the B3006 for Rake. Cross the A3 and look out on your right for a children's playground in the trees, just beyond the gate of Clayton Court. This is also the entrance to a beautiful wood, Durford Heath.

Durford Heath *790 260,* ♀, *62 acres, easy if dry, NT*
The sand road to the woods is like the neck of a flask – bear right or left for a circuit taking about $1\frac{1}{2}$ hours – if you don't linger. Like a flask or a bubble of pure ancient countryside in a great sea of forestry pines, this is a valley and a hill with many odd corners, quiet, and a place to get to know and love. Bearing left down the valley you go by a wood-bank with oaks grown up from old coppice stools. The hillside opposite is patterned with coppice oak and some birch. Deeper into the valley the wood becomes pure oak with large patches of bilberry. There are Scots pines above, apparently seeded from old plantations in Durford Wood to the west, which is private land, and from the gardens of large houses

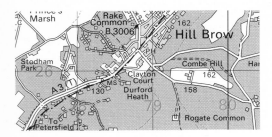

Oak and bilberry, Durford Heath

miles to the west. The ride remains from a grand avenue first planted on the last day of George III's reign in 1820, as an elegant tablet on the wall of the classical lodge cottage tells us. Two burly oaks nearby must be survivors. This is a walk with an unexpected architectural focus: the great house at the end of the avenue is prettily proportioned in red brick and white marble. In clear March sunlight the fine straight boles of beeches with their background of chestnut coppice shone in subtle variations of grey.

Hindhead and **Haslemere Commons**
Around Hindhead in Surrey is a record collection of National Trust commons totalling 1076 acres, and heavily wooded in parts. Just to the east is the famous Gibbet Hill, 895 feet with the Devil's Punchbowl on Hindhead Common below and across the A3(T). There is a parking ground at *891 358*, but the commons are all nearly continuous and accessible on foot from the village. To the north-west are Golden Valley and Whitmore Vale, 155 acres of wood and heath: to the south-east, Inval and Weydown Commons, these latter reaching to Haslemere. Nutcombe Down and Polecat Copse are to the south. Ludshott Common is in Hampshire, to the west beyond Grayshott, and includes Croaker's Patch, Gentle's Copse and Hammer Ponds at Waggoners Wells: in all 645 acres; then Bramshott Common is to the south, and across the A3 the woods of Hammer Bottom.

The best known of Haslemere's surrounding country is Black Down, 918 feet, 1½ miles south-east; there are 600 acres of National Trust land, with Tennyson's Lane and Boarden Door Bottom with a chestnut coppice. Black Down Hill is the highest point in Sussex, and Hindhead is the highest village in Surrey. The hills are sandstone and the vegetation heathland with birch and pine, bracken and heather. Views east and south to the Downs are filled with trees – enough to take your breath away at what seems the expanse of woodland.

Kingley Vale *825 088*, ♠ *(yew), about 3m, NR*
The map reference is for the parking place at

bordering the road. There seem to be no deer to eat the shoots, and oak stubs cut in the autumn already showed new shoots in March. No rabbits were to be seen, and few birds – this part of the country is curiously short of birds. The valley is a suntrap; all is quiet and windless. Nothing disturbs the pattern of warm oak bark, dry leaves and shiny green *Vaccinium*, and the very varied and satisfying shapes of all the trees.

To avoid the A3(T) and Petersfield (not that this little town is anything to avoid) head eastwards and then south to Rogate, Nyewood and South Harting, on the B2146 past Uppark (open April to September) to Compton and on to the Downs – a quiet country drive from the Weald sand to the considerable heights of the chalk hills. Turn right in West Marden for Forestside – a mere row of cottages – and left through **Stansted Forest**. Here the road is plentifully supplied with lay-bys, not very tidy ones. At Stansted House a footpath leaves the road at right angles, *754 104*, along a great ride by the side of a (private) wood. The path goes straight to Rowland's Castle, the village 1¼

guess at their age is 500 years, but they may be much older. There are no other plants in the wood, which is of course very dark and dry, but some clearings occur naturally, and here an occasional robin or chaffinch may be seen or heard. The Tansley Memorial Stone at the head of the vale commemorates the great man who, in the early years of this century, established the study of woodland ecology in Britain. His best-known book is *Britain's Green Mantle*. On the ridge are memorials to earlier men, supposedly Stone Age, who made their homes and their burial places here. It is difficult to believe that the yews were not here then, but it is quite possible that the Downs were bare and grazed by wild animals.

Juniper is the natural pioneer shrub of the chalk, and seedling yews require the shelter of juniper, which, when they grow up, they shade out. The yew is hospitable to man, but it is poisonous and an aggressive, intolerant and persistent tree. Old yews continually regroup their forces, sending up fresh trunks around the old, rotting wood and even setting seedlings in their own stumps. Long, drooping branches can root themselves, forming a ring of new trees around a parent.

The glossy leaflet produced by the Nature Conservancy tells, almost in Beatrix Potter style, how every autumn 2000 redwings and fieldfares come here from Scandinavia and gorge themselves on the yew berries for a month.

Grassland preservation is an important task of the Nature Conservancy in this area, and grazing is carefully controlled to keep the natural balance. The turf includes ten grasses and thirty flowering plants, among these stemless thistles and orchids.

Kingley Vale can also be reached by Stoughton Down, but this is a long way around if you want to spend time exploring the yews. A Forestry Commission car park at Lambdown Hill, *815 126*, in a field at the edge of the plantation, is strongly recommended in a Commission leaflet as secluded. But even in December about twenty cars occupied the gravel, and the grass was too slippery to drive on. To reach this parking place turn off the B2141 for East Marden, and then take the road to the south in the village.

West Stoke, near Mid Lavant just north of Chichester. The road to West Stoke is signposted Funtington from Mid Lavant. This very important site is a Nature Conservancy reserve. There is about a mile to walk – thank goodness you cannot drive into this one. First you come to a patch of chalk scrub with a field museum and leaflet dispenser. There are a lot of unnecessary notices along the very necessary fence. As the ground rises the yews begin. One outlier, perfect in form, is surrounded by a natural bank and shut in by tall grass and brambles. Within its shade you can easily imagine making a temporary home. Some shattered, dead yews become very visible at the edge of the wood. These were killed by war-time rifle practice, which stripped the thin bark.

Twenty very old yews are the parent trees to be found deep in the wood. A conservative

Micheldever Wood 529 364, ♣, *easy walk*, FC

1½ miles north to south, ¾ mile wide, this wood is east of the A33(T), 3 miles north of Winchester; turn off at Lunways Inn.

Old gnarled oaks and maples in the hedges, rectangular stands of beech, spruce, western red cedar within, are all on level ground. The main drive is gravelled and impressively lined with tall Norway spruces. This is an old wood converted into a timber factory, and in countryside which is given over to large-scale rural industries and main roads. Even so, the wood retains much beauty because of the various ages and the variety of trees, and the countryside round about has kept its breadth and grandeur.

The M3, as planned, will sweep the east flank of the wood, and this will probably destroy altogether its already threatened silence.

Yew and oak in close companionship, Abbotstone Down

Abbotstone Down 582 362, ♀, *picnic place*, CC

Three or 4 miles east of Micheldever Wood is Abbotstone Down, not primarily a woodland site. There are various parking places and picnic areas among trees and chalk scrub. Here a finger-post beckons walkers with seven-league boots north to Inkpen Beacon, many miles away near Newbury. Less energetically, you can wander on grassland between fine beeches, yews, birches, thorns, and inspect the edges of a fine oak/ash wood, rich in lichens and mosses, and open enough for a very varied field layer, including a good deal of privet – a chalk scrub plant and unusual as an undershrub for oak. Even in December, wood spurge and hairy St John's wort were recognizable, the first by its dark green lower leaves and the second by an extraordinary reddish-brown of the stalks and seeds, a colour which, strangely, did not show up on my Kodachrome film. These plants spread in newly cleared woodland and in some parts of the country are indicators of the ancient origin of the wood. This ground is fenced off and not for walking in; the floor is patterned with mossy, dead branches, the remains, presumably, of cleared coppice, and it ought to be left like that. Sadly, spruce has been planted. Outside the fence the grassy glades, perhaps formed originally by pasturing sheep, are perpetuated by the exploring feet of picnickers: the contrast is instructive. It looks as if there are no resident deer, because the 3-foot-high barbed wire would not keep them out, and there is no sign of grazing. Natural regeneration of shrubs and trees can thus continue and provide the varied habitats so desperately needed in our countryside; at least until the conifers take over. Look out for a fine spindle tree, about 200 yards along the bridleway southwards.

Chawton Park Wood 672 362, 2–3m, FC

This wood is off the A31, 3 miles south-west of Alton; turn north out of Four Marks, the first available turning if going south-west.

The first thing I saw was a group of roe deer; their white rumps bounced delicately away into the larches. Many dogs are walked here without leads in spite of a notice prohibiting this, and obviously the deer manage quite well. The parking place is practically within the village.

This wood is a triangle around a dry valley. There are old wood-banks, beeches and a pleasant wide picnic area within the wood, ½ mile from the car park. Conifers are larch and spruce.

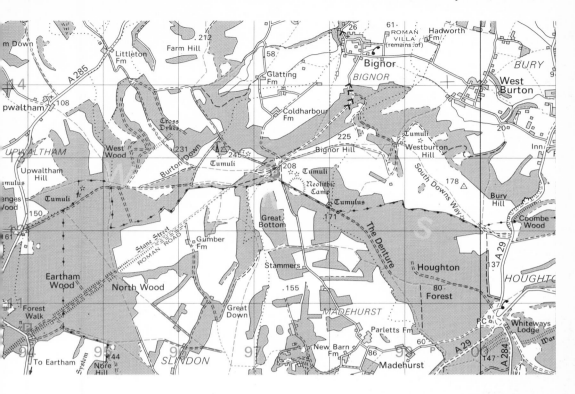

Bignor Hill 973 128

You can drive south from Bignor on a very steep road, but for a woodland approach turn towards Madehurst off the A29 immediately after the great roundabout on top of the Downs. Near a bit of a hazel coppice you can park, *994 104*, and walk gently uphill by the edge of Houghton Forest on a bridleway amusingly called 'The Denture'. Part of the way is bordered by silver firs, *Abies grandis*, which is agreeable. Try the foliage for its reputed scent of oranges. It is a long plod, with only an occasional dramatic view, which culminates in a patch of thorns belonging to the National Trust. Do we have to have the Trust preserve a few hawthorns, I asked myself? Then I came upon an open space dominated by a massive signpost pointing to Londinium one way and Noviomagus the other. At first I felt a bit scornful. There are a few yews, more signs; then I noticed Stane Street itself, a dead-straight dyke going off into the woods. As I stood upon this 1950-year-old

Signpost on the top of Bignor Hill

road, I began to see the point of the self-consciously Roman signpost.

You can descend via Madehurst by bearing right of your upward route, soon reaching a metalled lane. The countryside is beautifully shaped here. To the south at **Slindon** is National Trust woodland around Slindon Park and Common, with a small parking area at the north side, *955 085*.

Continuing south-west down Stane Street from Bignor Hill would bring you to **Eartham Wood**, a Forestry Commission conversion of oak into beech with Douglas fir at the centre and spruces round about. A nice enough place to park, *939 107*, and a pleasant walk, though far from exciting. The same could be said for **Selhurst Park Woods** just across the A285; there are two parking places on the Goodwood road with great views southwards, and another in the valley on the West Dean road.

West Dean Estate *872 111*

West Dean Estate has an arboretum marked on the map, by The Trundle viewpoint; a good place for cars to stop but with no apparent access to the woodlands. Beyond West Dean towards Chilgrove, you might park at the crossways at *846 147* for Westdean Woods: not a grand walk, on the bridleway, by a larchwood with ashes and open fields to the south, but pleasant and light. The estate is clearly carefully managed; a great stack of oak and chestnut logs shows that nothing is wasted. These downland oakwoods are not of course on chalk but on the deposits of clay-with-flints which lie over the chalk. Further into Westdean Woods is a young plantation of spruce, Douglas fir and western red cedar, with the seductive name of Venus Wood.

Singleton, on the A286, has a National Trust copse, and West Dean an open-air museum – open in summer.

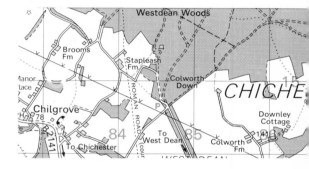

Bridleway at *846 147*, Westdean Woods

SOUTH-EAST ENGLAND
Surrey Hills and Wealden Forests

Landranger sheets 186, 187, 197

ASHDOWN FOREST

An area of forest ridges on Wealdon sand, it is well above the surrounding countryside and characteristic vegetation is heathland with birch and pine. 'Deer for six miles', warn notices on the roads. Ashdown Forest gets a good press nowadays, probably simply because it is geographically prominent. It is often cited as a survivor of Andreadsweald, though it might well have been a bald patch in that mighty oakwood. Arthur Young, 1741–1820, wrote that it was '18,000 acres of nothing better than the poorest barren sand, the vegetable covering consisting of ferns, heath etc' – but he was a horticulturalist. Tradition has it that the many iron furnaces of Sussex (32 on record in the sixteenth century) were responsible for the loss of many trees but this is

unlikely. All the trees would regenerate after cutting, and we should have been left with even thicker forest. It was the grazing animals of the commoners which polished off the trees.

Ashdown Forest, ever since it was first called a forest in the time of Henry III, has been the source of much besides mere timber and firewood: its relatively open glades were a wood-pasture and its moorland provided turves; its heather and even its bracken were valued for litter; the sandy hills were no doubt full of rabbits from the time of the introduction of that beast in the twelfth century, and there would be game for the taking. All these demands from the ordinary people who lived there were at variance with those of the owners of the hunting rights – at first the King, then the Duchy of Lancaster and later various lords who competed for the Mastership. Clearly it

Ashdown Forest birches

was worth having. 7000 acres were enclosed in the early eighteenth century, and other parts were sold, but the commoners continued to assert their traditional rights until a Keeper of the Forest in the mid-nineteenth century, Lord de la Warre, attempted to restrain them legally. He lost his case and the forest of some 6000 acres is now managed by a body representative of the commoners.

The conservators have provided many car parks in the Wych Cross area, grouped along the ridge road (un-numbered) west to east, or the A22 running south (where in the valley you may find mature beechwoods).

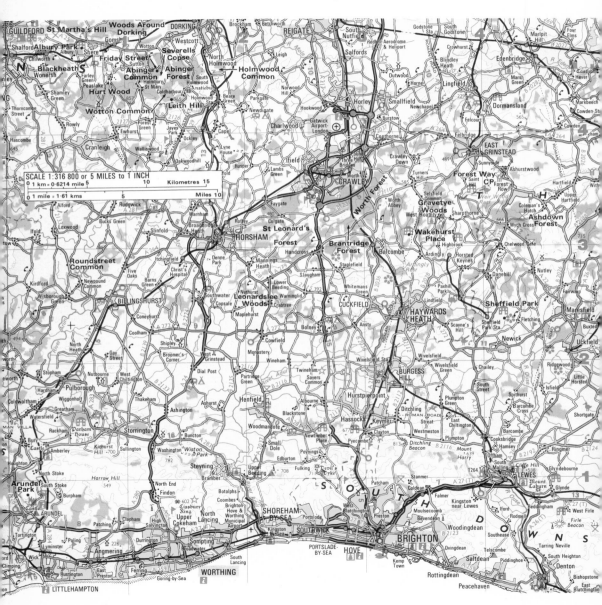

Grazing is not now a major concern, so birch and pine are spreading through the heather, some of which is cut in wide lanes. There are footpaths everywhere. I have not discovered a strictly woodland walk here. The heath is to be enjoyed for its openness, but there are patches of graceful birchwood, some oaks, and striking groups of pine.

Gravetye Woods 360 350, ♀ ♠, 1½m, muddy, FC

At the north-west edge of Ashdown Forest, the Forestry Commission has taken over a fine plantation which is credited to William Robinson, a great gardener. The parking place is discreet, not too easy to find: turn off the B2110, 2 miles south-west of East Grinstead where the road turns sharply to the right. Conifers at Gravetye are almost mature but nicely contrasted; a stand of Serbian spruce is particularly fine. There are helpful signposts and a path to a viewpoint above the woods. There are many native trees.

Forest Way CP 425 356, ♀, 2½m, easy but wet in places, CC

From Forest Row to East Grinstead runs the Forest Way Country Park, beginning inauspiciously at the bottom of a hill on a main road, the A22. There is nowhere to park at this end. This Forest Way is an old railway, mostly in a cutting and not too well drained. Its

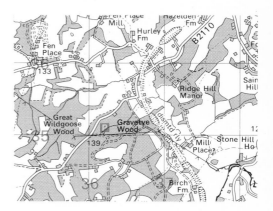

Serbian spruce and Corsican pine, Gravetye Woods

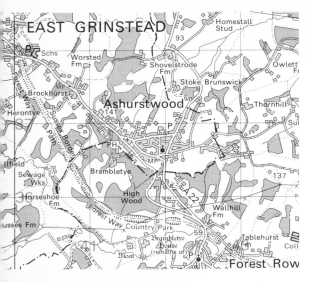

charms are slow to yield on a wet November afternoon: nevertheless they are there. At one point you pass by a particularly charming beech coppice, guarded by a guelder rose. There are many field maples. At another point you find wooden steps to encourage you to walk on the bank top, where, from the dignified cover of a row of old thorns, you survey the rolling, wooded landscape to the south.

Sheffield Park *403 237*, ♀ ♠, *arboretum, NT*

Another dismantled railway through East Grinstead has been for some of its length rebuilt as the Bluebell Line. This is a woodland and arable 'walk' by steam train, from Horsted Keynes, *371 292*, to its southern terminus, Sheffield Park.

There is no woodland here as such, though the great size and vigour of the many specimen conifers at Sheffield Park make a semblance of woodland. The park is an accumulation of enthusiasms from Capability Brown's planning of lakes, grass and 'clumps', to exotic-tree collecting by A. G. Soames, the owner from 1909. The park has been in the care of the National Trust since 1954. The design seems aimed at a splendid explosion of non-greens in autumn, but it is a superb place to visit at any time, except that it is only open sporadically after mid November until May. This would be rather late for *Magnolia kobus* while you would miss the flowers of *Parrotia persica* altogether – both are specialities here. *Nyssa sylvatica*, the tupelo tree, was planted in quantity in 1909 and forms a stand unique in the country. There are fine examples of rare conifers: *Athrotaxis, Saxegothaea, Pseudolarix* (the golden larch) and Montezuma pine. There are palms, ornamental bridges, water-lilies and ducks.

Wakehurst Place *340 315*, ♀ ♠, *arboretum, NT*

North of Sheffield Park on the B2028, about 1 mile north of Ardingly, is Wakehurst Place, National Trust but leased to the Royal Botanic Gardens at Kew, which is a branch of the Ministry of Agriculture, Fisheries and Food.

Palms and conifers by the lake in Sheffield Park

Open every day, hot water laid on, invalid chairs available, special policemen to take your money, and well worth every penny.

There is a 'wooded walk' between steep cliffs, a Himalayan valley with, of course, rhododendrons – but you may never reach it because there is so much else to see. If you *can't* get far there is plenty to see, and smell, near the house, where exemplary rock gardens dip down to perfect lawns. If it is hot you can pause under a very large small-leaved lime, or promenade below *Davidia* and *Cupressus macrocarpa* of truly forest proportions – in the latter case probably much bigger than in their native, windswept Monterey. You may plunge through long grass to see the most amazingly large Australian cider gums (*Eucalyptus gunnii*) knee-deep in their own peeling bark.

The pinetum, an open woodland in itself, is a mile beyond the house; grand, soberly laid out, well labelled. Most of its specimens are old, and all you see is a piece of trunk, with its pattern of leaves far overhead. This is often the difficulty with old specimen conifers, but at least the ground is clear. I was delighted to find the not-too-common Spanish or hedgehog fir hiding in a corner near the stables, quite

Hedgehog fir (*Abies pinsapo*), Wakehurst Place

friendly and approachable. You can have tea at the house; the house is lovely too. There is a small museum display of local natural history.

ST LEONARD'S FOREST

St Leonard's Forest is more or less between Crawley and Horsham. Cobbett wrote:

> The first two of these miserable miles go through the estate of Lord Erskine. It was a *bare heath* with here and there, in the better parts of it, some scrubby *birch*. It has been in part planted with fir-trees which are as ugly as the heath was; and in short, it is a most villainous tract. After quitting it we went through a *forest*; but a most miserable one; and this is followed by a large common, *now enclosed*, cut up, disfigured, spoiled, and the labourers all driven from its skirts. I have seldom travelled over eight miles so well calculated to fill the mind with painful reflections. The ride has, however, this in it; that the ground is pretty much elevated and enables you to look about you.

Nowadays there are rather more *firs* (Scots pine) and larches but the labourers are as little in evidence. Rides are blocked with warning notices and even pieces of old motor car, an item this part of the world is not short of. St Leonard, you might imagine, was the patron saint of real estate.

Things get a little better to the south, where the plantations thin out among narrow fields. At Lower Grouse you may walk into the woods and even buy an ice-cream at the farm, *234 308*. The chief reason for visiting this part might be to see the great Hammer Pond and Hawkins Pond, where energy was stored to work drop-hammers forging the local iron. Hammer Pond appears to be inaccessible, but Hawkins has the Forestry Commission Old Copse, *218 295*, on its east bank – rather thickly planted but you can park and walk in: refrain from blocking the gateway with your car. There is a scattering of native trees along the waterside, and they look very pretty against the background of dark conifers. Access on the far bank is for the fishermen only, but there is a bridleway – very muddy in winter – a few yards along the road. It fails to afford a view of the pond, but proceeding by beeches in parkland it heads north into the forest for 2 miles, eventually reaching Colgate. All I found at Colgate's Beacon Hill was not a view but a colossal tip with a list of charges. Perhaps I should have looked further, but when I detect a certain aura, nothing can persuade me to walk on. All I will say is that the bridleway heads into the forest. I headed the other way, to Leonardslee.

Leonardslee Woods and Furnace Pond
222 259, ♀ (♣), *easy, muddy 1–3m*
The famous gardens of Leonardslee at Lower Beeding are not open all the year, but a little way south along the A281 is a lane, Mill Lane, labelled as a public bridleway. You can drive (carefully, there are children) down the lane where you can just about park a car and then

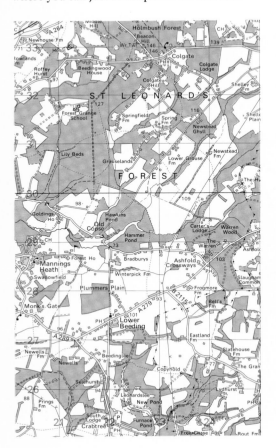

walk into the estate woodlands. Here you can see the Furnace Pond, a much better example, if smaller, than the Hammer Pond mentioned above. The original dam has been decorated with a beech hedge, whose contorted branches are reminiscent of the ancient old beeches in the grounds, pollarded many decades ago. The ruined walls of some of the foundry buildings can be seen, and a deeply hollowed cart track winds out of the valley to nowhere in particular. The stream below the dam has been made into another lake at a lower level.

The woodlands are a strange, neglected mixture, a little depressing but fascinating too. A noble fir, whose proportions suggest the full 150 years possible, and some Lawson cypress, form a western American enclave, while quite close by is a beech whose heavy, complex form is surely the result of lopping over a century ago. On the valley sides I found a holly whose roots are combined with those of a larger oak, and not far away a similar mating of beech with oak. A large larch of apparently excellent timber quality has been allowed to fall, and dead wood is everywhere. The woodland here is probably only seen as a neutral background to the great garden.

Once beyond the valley of the Furnace Pond and out to the east, you have a choice of footpaths and bridleways. There appears to be a right of way to the drive of Lydhurst, which is a very up-stage sort of house. A left turn in the larchwood brings you back below the high-tension wires to Beedinglee or you may pick up the old Furnace road out to the B2115. Several footpaths are signposted, but the great meadow called Copyhold has a new owner, so maybe some changes will be attempted.

A car park at *207 298*, off the A281, gives access to 13 acres of nature reserves near Lower Beeding, including the beechwood, Mick's Cross.

To the north of St Leonard's Forest, off the A264 and close to the new estate of Broadfield is a local country park, **Buchan Park**, *248 336*: useful perhaps if you are desperate to get away from the incessant traffic of Crawley and its M23, or have just landed at Gatwick and need to recover from jetlag. Crawley has crept over Pease Pottage Forest and Tilgate Forest, so we go further south on the A23 and turn left onto the B2110 – for Brantridge Forest.

Brantridge Forest *289 316, ♀ ♠, 500 yards, easy, can be wet, fp*

A great notice about fire danger marks the start, through a gap in the hedge, of a woodland walk *par excellence* and an experience of deep significance for anyone who can be moved by the dramatic but very, very slow response of beech trees to men's saws and axes. Some will only say, 'grotesque!' Others, like me, will not so much walk as hover, unable to remove their eyes, yet led on to seek out the next revelation. It is the cumulative effect of a double avenue of these strange creatures which is so extraordinary, compared with the more scattered effect of the similar Burnham

Beeches. The trees were planted here long before they were lopped, and what we now see is a complete, probably quite unintentional collaboration between the planter, the woodmen, and the trees which have outlived them. This passionate scene gives way soon enough to bracken, birches and pine. Further on northwards into **Worth Forest**, the Paddockhurst Estate has made a parking place, *305 332*, now full of puddles, and invites you, on your best behaviour, to explore the geometrical rides of its conifer plantations.

WOODS NEAR DORKING

Box Hill (see p. 90) is the best known but by no means the most important of Dorking's woodlands. A clockwise survey takes us south through Brockham and right at the crossroads

Ancient pollard beeches, Brantridge Forest

1½ miles towards Newdigate, where the Forestry Commission has a small wood, **High Ridge**, with a parking place, *199 470*: nothing special but a nice mixture of conifers, including the bewitchingly scented *Thuja plicata*. A sad pond surrounded by oaks and willows tells the tale of another wood, its heart ripped out and replaced with alien trees – but no doubt it was all felled during the Second World War and would have become arable were it not for the intervention of the Forestry Commission – the usual excuse.

Holmwood Common *184 453*, ♀, *632 acres, various routes, muddy at times, NT*

The indicated parking place is by a pond at the crossroads ¼ mile east of South Holmwood.

Half a dozen perpetually hungry Chinese geese live on the pond. The path leads confusingly to an access road serving some grand houses, notably the Old Croft in Edwardian red brick. The part of the common I explored was very pretty woodland with oak, holly, yew, mature birch, planted larches and invading sycamores. The central part of the common is mostly east of the A24 about 2 miles south of Dorking. But there is a great deal more woodland to see on the west side of that road.

Abinger Forest, Leith Hill, Abinger and **Wotton Commons** ♀ ♠, *CC, NT*

A very large area of hilly country with a great variety of woodland extremely well preserved. Enchanted Abinger! Barely 30 miles from

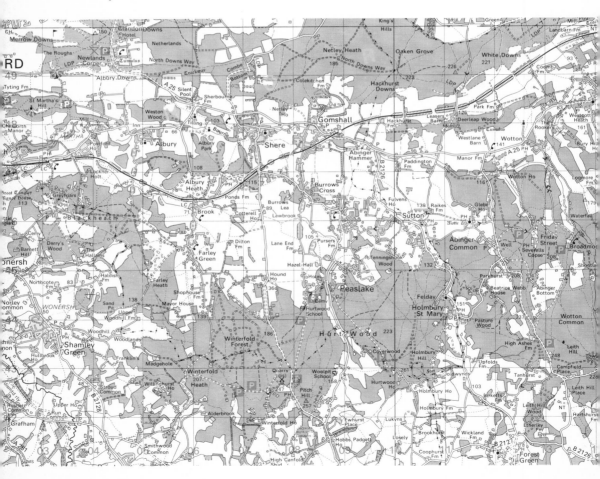

London, and yet as remote as County Kerry – almost. At a parking place near **Friday Street**, *126 457*, you may plunge at once into a vast community of drunken oaks awash in a sea of bilberry and often covered in green moss. Soon you are aware of very tall, straight pines – good timber trees with a canopy high above the oaks which still writhe in its shade. Let us hope that the oaks will survive the removal, surely imminent, of the pines.

This part, Abinger Common with the adjoining Wotton Common, is administered by Surrey County Council and remains in private ownership. It can only have survived through the care and foresight of the owners, for we all know the type of development which might have occurred.

Beyond Friday Street, which is a sweet little place in a wooded cleft filled by a wide hammer pond, lies another gem, **Severells Copse**. This is a birch coppice with old oaks, National Trust, and seductively beautiful. You can cross it by a well-marked path to another Surrey County Council car park on the ridge, *134 454*, beyond which lie Wotton Common and Abinger Forest to the south and east, respectively. I cannot tell you which way to go, but I avoided the more coniferized eastern parts. South is Leith Hill, the highest point in south-east England, and below it a good deal of National Trust property, including Ralph Vaughan Williams' Leith Hill Place, now an estate run by traditional methods, Tanners Wood, Ockshott Wood (now cut down), Mosses Wood with its landslip; and all with great views southwards over the Weald.

The eastern shoulder of the forest is coniferized and contains the Forestry Commission's Bury Hill Wood and Redlands Wood.

Hurtwood *070 440*, ♣, *pf*

Nearer to Guildford, though still equidistant from Dorking, lies Hurtwood, a forest or a collection of manorial wastes consisting largely of heathland with pines and birches: tall beechwoods at the southern escarpment edge. As with Abinger and Wotton Commons, which almost adjoin, the greensand dip slope is broken by deep north-to-south valleys, here containing not hammer ponds but seasonal streams, not persistent enough to waterlog the remaining oak trees. Rich homesteads, parks and farmland border the southern slopes, where monkey puzzles, Lawson cypresses and rhododendron are added to the prevailing tall beeches. Coppice trees are less evident here – when the land was abducted or enclosed, there were probably few commoners to stand up for their rights. As long ago as the twelfth century, the Surrey knights paid 200 marks to King Richard, 'to be quit of all things that belong to the Forest from the waters of Wey to Kent, and from the street of Guildford southwards as far as Surrye stretches'. Now the woodland is dedicated to the public and managed by the Lords of the Manors, who have banded

TOP: Abinger Forest from Ranmore Common
CENTRE: Beeches on a south-facing slope of
Leith Hill
ABOVE: Abinger Common oaks
RIGHT: An old yew in Severells Copse

themselves into the sinister-sounding Hurtwood Control.

The impression you get at any of the fourteen or more parking places provided is that you had better be careful. And, so you had. Hurtwood is a national asset as well as a source of good pine timber. At the north-west there is a square mile called Winterfold Forest which is heavily coniferized by the Forestry Commission. There are viewpoints along the south escarpment and a pub, the Windmill, below the intersection of the two main lanes from Gomshall and Shere.

As woodland, Hurtwood is a little relentless, better riding country than walking. But if you start from a central parking place and walk east or west across the grain of the countryside you can be sure of vigorous exercise, while clear views from high ground, especially in clearings, help you to keep your bearings. In winter the strong red colour of the ever-present bracken contrasts with the full green of the Scots pine. There are also birch, oak and beech, with heather on older banks. Pines regenerate naturally. Leaves of bilberry persist bright green well into the winter. It is from these berries, once collected and sold, that Hurtwood gets its name. Hurts – the name whortleberry is only a corruption of hurtlebury – were once collected and sold like cherries. Bilberry jam is excellent but apparently now only imported from Poland.

South of the A25 is **Albury Park**, *062 475*, once the home of our first man of the trees, John Evelyn.

Only 2 miles south-east of Guildford is **Blackheath**, *040 462*, with a Surrey County Council parking place and a 20-acre National Trust section of pine and heather. This is just south-east of Chilworth, while to the north of that place is **St Martha's Hill**, with the Pilgrims' Way emerging from suburban Guildford onto the chalk hill with its viewpoint, *028 482*.

Sydney Wood, between Dunsfold and Alfold, can be entered, but it is a plantation at present not organized for public access. There are, however, rights of way through it from west to east, guarded at each end by imposing

Pine and oak, Hurtwood

private houses, and from north to south. The southern exit could be difficult and flooded in winter.

To get away from even the benign Surrey County Council and Forestry Commission on to informal footpaths in heavily wooded farmland, turn off the B2133 at **Roundstreet Common**. Here are footpaths leading off right and left into interesting country marked by the 'Wey South Path', in a not-quite-dry disused navigation channel – in fact quite impassable and whole fields wide in a wet December.

From here, or from Hurtwood or Leith Hill, you can retire on the very beautiful village of Ockley on a section of Stane Street (see Bignor Hill, p. 23); here it is the A29. Just south of Ockley turn right and then twice left via Standon Homestead for Okewood church. This was a Chapel of Ease, a forest chapel in the thirteenth century; it was rebuilt in the fifteenth. Here we are once again in the grey/brown/green crepuscular mediaeval atmosphere of the forest. A short woodland walk upstream from the churchyard brings you to Walliswood (which has a pub) and back to the twentieth century.

Arundel Park *022 083*
Half a mile out of Arundel under the castle cliff is a large parking place for the Wildfowl Reserve. Here begins Walk No 1 of the Arun Valley Walks designed by West Sussex County Council: leaflet 'usually available'. The leaflet was not available when I visited, but the notice-board map assured me that the longest

walk would take $1\frac{3}{4}$ hours; 3 hours later I had achieved an abbreviated circuit, though I must admit to several long pauses.

Instead of slogging around Offham and South Stoke, if you ascend to the trees via the old quarry you will find yourself in a corner of Arundel Park. Sheltered by tall spruces is a box grove. Some of these box trees are remarkably straight and thick, and it is tragic to see how they have been allowed to fall to the ground. The air here was still, in spite of a gale blowing in the Channel not far away, and a boxwood is always an attractive place, but to me it was like a mortuary full of decaying corpses. The present price of boxwood for engraving is 35 pence per square inch, medium quality. The end grain is used, so that the size of the blocks is limited to the girth of the tree. But each of these trunks has a potential value of £200–£300.

Emerging from the park wall via a large hole, you can cross a field and pick up a bridleway by Fox's Oven Cottage, and then left to the small wood of that name, very much a mixed wood of conifers and broadleaves. A short walk along the road towards South Stoke brings you to a lane leading direct to one of the park gates. Inside, a steep ascent, partly by chalky paths, brings you to a bench-mark at 347 feet, and from here you can return by the sides of mature beech 'clumps', with great views of the castle and the sea, down to Swanbourne Lake. Not entirely a woodland walk, but very invigorating, among magnificent beeches.

The flooded Arun from Arundel Park

THE KENTISH WEALD AND THE SOUTH DOWNS

Bedgebury Forest, 3500 acres dominates our map north-east of Flimwell, *716 315*. It is 45 miles from London on the A21(T), the wood-land road. Its mighty folds of green, like a rug thrown over the Garden of England, can be seen from the Flimwell to Hawkhurst road. Turn north at Hawkhurst onto the B2085 to enter the forest at Tubslake: or you can walk in at the Royal Oak, Flimwell. Buses stop here from London's Victoria Bus Station or from Tunbridge Wells.

The forest is important, if only because of its size. There are now:

120 acres Corsican pine
150 acres larch (Japanese, European and
    Dunkeld, their hybrid)
120 acres Norway spruce
80 acres Douglas fir
240 acres oak and other hardwoods

In addition are 4 acres of Lawson cypress and 1 acre of Japanese cedar. This last is very unusual as a forest tree in Britain, but important in Japan.

The rides seem endless if you are in a hurry, but of course it is ridiculous to be in a hurry. There are dozens of routes through: you need a compass really, but there are some signposts.

Bedgebury Pinetum *718 337,* ♀ ♣,
80 acres parkland, many routes, FC

Few people with an interest in trees will spend long in the forest itself, for at the north-west corner is the National Pinetum. Turn off the A21 where signposted to Goudhurst and Bedgebury. The car park is enormous, with the expected Forestry Commission services and a fine centrepiece of *Cotoneaster* where many sparrows wait to share your lunch. The **Churchill Wood** walk, close at hand, is short, sheltered, easy and pleasant for the very old and the young. To see the beauties of the Pinetum itself, you have to be prepared for a moderately stiff walk downhill and up. There is a charge, voluntary in winter.

A pinetum is, of course, a collection of what

Bedgebury Pinetum: Hills Avenue, looking to Cypress Valley

used to be called Pinaceae, now the conifers, yews, *Ginkgo* and *Torreyas* (nutmeg trees) which make up the tree Gymnosperms. These (naked seed plants) are a very ancient class. They evolved about 350 million years ago, give or take a few tens of millions of years. Conifers were at their height of world dominance about 250 million years ago and were nearly equalled 100 million years later by the Ginkgoales, only one species of one genus of one family of the whole order of which survived: *Ginkgo biloba*, worthy of respect if only for its uniqueness. There are still over 500 species of conifers and several Taxaceae (yews and nutmeg trees).

Angiosperms, including all the familiar flowering plants and broadleaved trees (hardwoods), have evolved over the past 140 million years, along with the mammals and the declining, but still very strong, Coniferales to which this pinetum is dedicated.

Although it is a sort of living museum, the Pinetum strikes one first and foremost as a landscape; not a wild one, but certainly a happy place for any lover of trees. Here the conifers you knew as interesting specimens or all-too-familiar windbreaks can be seen in their true form and vigour. Massed with the skill of a great designer (his name was W. Dallimore, a botanist retired from Kew and no rich lord), the great avenues sweep along shallow valleys or leap across small, rounded hills, with a constantly changing architecture of trees. The soil is said to be poor, but great *Thujas* and *Tsugas*, remarkably rich-looking *Cryptomeria* and *Sciadopitys* flourish, and the cleverly grouped large specimens of Lawson cypress in their two dozen or so different forms and colours are an eye-opener. The juniper section, immediately opposite the entrance, is enlightening; so is the Spruce Valley collection – much wider than elsewhere. Firs and Douglas firs are said to be failures at Bedgebury, but I think they call anything a failure that is not perfectly formed and 75 feet high since 1925. The older pines and firs were very short of labels in 1982 (apparently people steal labels). Bedgebury is not a good place for the Chinese firs. The rainfall is 33 inches a year as against 85 inches in the west of Scotland.

The Forest Plots beyond the pinetum area

are of course for instruction, not for beauty. But straight rides do not a prison make, and I for one can muse happily there for hours, re-assured when botany deserts me by the well-placed labels and the diagram – an example of efficient forestry graphics – in the excellent booklet available at the office. Broadleaved trees are in the minority, but those species present are interesting and they gain from their isolation amongst the dark green of the conifers. Not all conifers, of course, remain green through the winter. One of the sights of Bedgebury in the autumn is the dignified, simple group by the lake of swamp cypress and dawn redwood, alternately coloured in two shades of red: the former dark, the latter glowing and light, and by November surrounded by an unbelievable carpet of its strange, feathery leaves.

Scots pine and, beyond, oriental spruce in the Forest Plots at Bedgebury

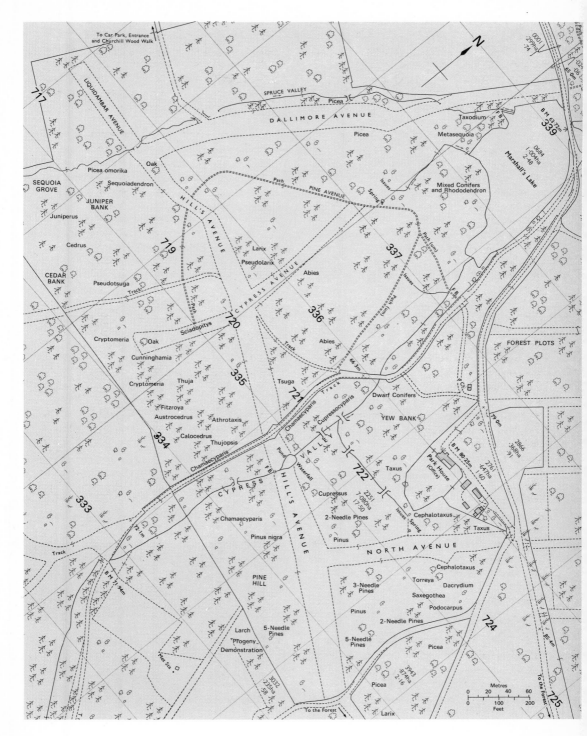

Chingley Wood: standard oaks and coppiced chestnut

Chingley Wood *676 338, ♀ ♣, 2m, easy, WA*

On the opposite side of the A21(T) from Bedgebury is Bewl Bridge Reservoir, with a special turning 1 mile south of Lamberhurst. The woodlands here, notably Chingley Wood, are of native trees, with pines planted in the last century. There is a very tidy car park which demands a fairly high charge in 10-pence pieces; when visited in November it was deserted. The smart Visitors' Centre was open, and empty, except for one lonely trout in a glass tank. He seemed to be quite happy. There is a telephone, of course, and full life-saving equipment all round the water's edge. The resident flock of Canada geese took off like a formation of heavy bombers as the first hair of my head appeared over the dam wall.

Chingley Wood is fenced off, but if you persist you get to a footpath which strikes through, along an ancient bank with old hollies and beeches, birchwood to the right, chestnut coppice with fine native oaks to the left. The coppice is cut, but the wood seems to be left around to rot: rather more than might be necessary for conservation of insect life. You can walk on to Chingley Manor and out to the main road along the Manor drive, which is clearly marked on the map as a footpath. You emerge at The Happy Eater, but this leaves you a good 2 miles of roadway back to the car park and it is better to return through the wood. Notice the very large beech stumps at the water's edge: useless to speculate on the character of the valley that has been flooded.

But whatever the loss to the trees, the gain to bird life has been immense. The leaflet available at the Visitors' Centre lists no less than seventy waterfowl, shore birds and other water birds that have been seen at Bewl Bridge.

Pembury Walks *626 426, ♀ ♣, several hilly fps, LA*

Indicated by a finger-post on the A21(T), Pembury Walk is close to Tunbridge Wells. It sounds like a good place for a woodland walk, and so it proves, but in the plural. Effectively a vast ragged triangle of assorted forestry with a waterworks as the apex and the A21 as the base, it is an easy place to get lost in. The contorted, hilly land and the numerous paths, bridleways and rides not on the map make it confusing. Choose a sunny day or take a compass, because trying to guide yourself by the sound of the main road just does not work.

There is some space to park near the waterworks, *626 426*, or near the squat-towered, charming old Pembury church. Even the large hospital on the main road is rather short of parking space, and Tunbridge Wells Borough Council, who seem to be the landowners, would do well to construct a parking place for the woods, off the A21: no doubt there are plans.

Two footpaths leave the vicinity of the waterworks. The upper one travels between tall wire fences for all the world as if it were on the border of Russia: fine tall larches reinforce this impression. Soon there appear the old oak stubs, sculptured into complexity by frequent cutting and decay, that are typical of all the

Cleft chestnut and birch break, Pembury Walks

miles of wood-banks that surround the Pembury woods. There is a great deal of chestnut, some very old stools 6 feet wide at least, a lot of larch of various ages, and stands of younger Corsican pine.

All these appear as you follow the wire-fenced path as far as the cemetery, then turn right across the grain of the country to emerge near the hospital. Not too promising! And the way back is not clear from here. It is easy to get lost trying to reach the opposite side of the triangle. So, take the lower of the two paths at the waterworks and later strike off right to reach the road and return, is my advice, based I must admit on inadequate knowledge of the ground.

There is a great deal to see, all perhaps monotonously silvicultural, but rarely dull. At stream valley bottoms alder, birch and sycamore are coppiced along with the interminable, but variously aged, chestnut; sheltered corners of larchwoods make attractive places to rest. On ridges the paths are on yellow sand between pines; on slopes they show the pale grey clay of the Weald. Three-legged 'breaks' of birch poles nailed together

stand about in recently cut chestnut coppice, left by the paling makers. The chestnut leaves on one or two years' growth are a rich gold colour long after other leaves are gone, a more brilliant tint than the mustardy yellow of the larch. There is heather, broom and bracken, and the felted green of cowslip leaves in the coppices.

It is old woodland, as the oak stubs tell, but full of new life and reflecting a lively management policy that cannot be a bad thing. Pembury Walks only lack a few corners of high forest.

Friston Forest *545 000, ♀ ♣, 1967 acres, moderately easy trails and walks, FC*
The forest is near the Seven Sisters cliffs west of Eastbourne; 1967 acres ranging from 12 to 300 feet above sea-level. There is a network of bridleways and footpaths, and the Forestry Commission has provided three parking places. Turn off the A259 to Exceat or to Westdean or, in Friston, onto the B2105 for Butchershole Bottom, *557 005*. Whatever *that* name means the name Friston almost certainly means

Friston Forest

'furzetun', and furze or gorse is the native vegetation. Unbelievably, gorse, the prickliest of native bushes, was once an important resource as winter fodder, bedding instead of straw, and rapid fuel for firing bread ovens and potteries. This scrub was cleared by the foresters, who also took over some more level agricultural land where the thin soil suffered from erosion. Planting began in 1926, but most of the trees are much younger than this.

The forest walk from Westdean parking place ascends by easy gradients along the ride, where Corsican pine, very bright green here because of the chalky soil, is used to nurse the staple tree, the beech. The nurses are now being removed. The aim is to produce a great beechwood, not a mere catch crop of softwood in this the South Downs Area of Outstanding Natural Beauty. Here and there are hints of the grandeur that is to follow in time; now all is clear and simple – a teenage forest, and the

smooth haunches of the Downs complete this impression. As the sun reaches into Westdean village an older, richer pattern is revealed, a sheltered richness to contrast with the wind-polished purity of the chalk slopes. Friston Forest does not quite fit in with this theme, but it will in time, and there is plenty of bare grassland still. The trail of $2\frac{3}{4}$ miles marches with a branch of the long-distance path or South Downs Way for some of the way.

A shorter walk starts from the parking place nearest the main road, at Exceat, with views of the gleaming meanders of Cuckmere River. At Butchershole you are more sheltered, and on your own as regards trails: at any point in the forest you are free to wander. The land is a watershed for the Eastbourne waterworks, and afforestation is a sensible use of it. Rabbits caused a lot of problems at first by eating all the seedlings, and the soil is difficult. The leaflet claims 350 species of plants and

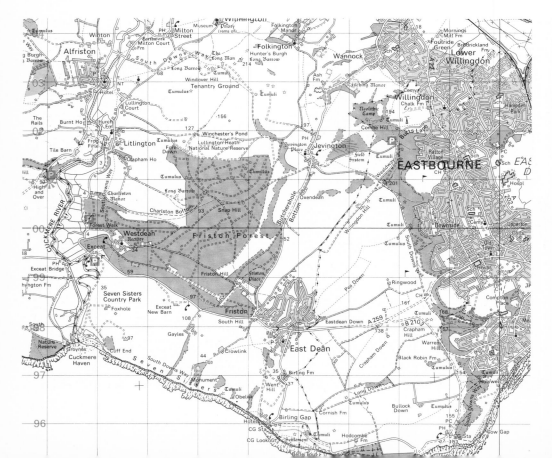

mentions viper's bugloss, traveller's joy and slender speedwell; the last of these has spread along the rides as a result of summer mowing. The marbled white butterfly is found here, along with the chalkhill blue and the Adonis blue: the first feeds on grasses and the blues on vetch, particularly horseshoe vetch, which grows in the chalk grassland. There are dew-ponds within the forest formed in pockets of clay over the chalk.

Woodland, mostly ash and sycamore, lines the precipitous western rampart of Eastbourne's suburbia. The South Downs Way runs from Westdean to Jevington and up again to this ridge, whence many footpaths descend to the streets. One amazing road, Butts Lane, from near the flintstone Post Office of Ratton Village, climbs to a car park at the top. Here you can observe the gorse scrub in quantity and drink in the heady air of 600 feet. A clump of beeches here looks a little bit

threadbare. **Lullington Heath**, *546 018*, which you can see beyond Jevington and north of Friston Forest is a National Nature Reserve.

Abbot's Wood *565 077*, ♀ ♠, *forest trail and disabled trail, FC*
A few miles inland at Abbot's Wood the Forestry Commission, with a leaflet, again invites you to examine your heritage. Perhaps it is not the Commission's fault, but most of the interest here seems to be outside or on the edges, where ancient wood-banks still support the fantastic and elegant shapes of many-stemmed coppice trees – hornbeams as well as oak and beech – many covered in ivy. A few oldish oaks still stand in the fields but most were felled during the Second World War. The Abbots were of Battle, until the Dissolution, and their men made the banks, cutting trees every twenty years or so and carting the wood away for fuel. In Victorian times coppice oak

Trees at Westdean, November

was cut and stacked to dry, the bark removed in 'flows' for the tanning industry. In the forest there is still some chestnut, and many old dead oak stools under the pines – I cannot help feeling our heritage lies with them. But the parking place offers all-important space – and more, for a walk has been arranged here for those confined to wheelchairs. Various organizations have donated trees, planted by the way – and more could be done here for the blind, in the form of bushes to touch and smell.

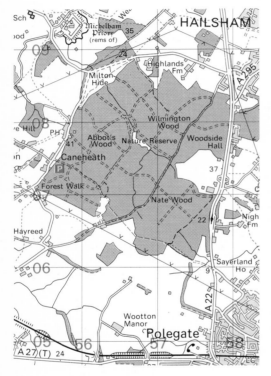

Footland Wood 763 203, ♀ ♠, 1¼ miles, easy, FC

North of Battle, this is a small wood among many in this area. The forest walk is short, the first half coniferous, the second through a beechwood. The older beeches are considered unsatisfactory, having come from poor seed, but if the day is dark you would do well to aim for them, taking the walk in reverse. Much as I admire the western hemlock for its generous, rich green cloak, these crowded stands of

equal-age timber strike me as gloomy. They are the battery hens of the woodlands. However, the Forestry Commission has placed a rustic seat for visitors to sit and admire them.

Light at the edges of the wood reveals the ancient character of the wood-banks, the trees once lopped and woven into the hedge. They are mainly beech, though this was originally an oakwood with birch, cut for the iron furnaces once concentrated in the Sussex Weald. These grotesque and yet graceful trees remind us of what we have lost. Their timber, of course, would be fit for only the most imaginatively carved constructions. Today's trees have been redesigned by the Industrial Revolution; whether for pulping or building they have to be straight. We cannot imagine even a wooden spoon being anything but strictly geometrical, but beech was used not long ago for a great range of household utensils now made of china, steel or plastic. Treen, it was called: spoons, bowls, forks; and beech is still the best timber for carved pieces like butter-pats, brush backs, rolling pins – not to mention chair legs, a subject on its own. Tools such as planes, small mallets and spokeshaves are still made of beech, as are some of the best toys. If no beech was available, birch, sycamore or elm was used. Large pieces like malt shovels and saddle trees were carved in one piece from split logs. But it is not difficult to imagine the branches and boles of these hedge trees being adapted to objects of use, well shaped to the human hand. It is quite possible that, one day, valuable furniture will be made, not symmetrical, not straight, but beautifully finished from these odd, increasingly rare coppice and hedge trees.

If you come in spring, you may find some flowers of the 140 species of plant mentioned in the leaflet, available for a small fee from a dispenser at the car park. I found some interesting puff balls.

Barne's Wood on the other side of the B2089 also belongs to the Forestry Commission. Chestnut coppice lines the road. To the east and beyond Cripp's Corner along the same road there is a vast area of woodland belonging to the Southern Water Authority. Every entrance is marked private except for one, *804 206*, where there is space to park and a public

Woodland walk in Footland Wood

footpath leading southwards, roughly along the line of high-tension pylons. The path begins on a double-tracked forest road, past a neat notice saying that it is not a public bridleway but an unofficial pony trail. The going is not too muddy. This is a mixed wood, such as is mentioned on Ordnance Survey maps but rarely seen; nice and open with occasional distant views over the reservoir which remains hidden below. There are oaks, some self-promoted from ancient stools, a lot of slightly ragged larch, some beech, some sycamore – all growing very straight in spite of not being regimented or all planted at once. The path takes a sharp turn eastwards, then continues more or less south for a mile or so to a wide opening used by tractors removing timber. This is on a narrow by-road which bounds the east side of the wood. This opening may be a better place to park at weekends – on working days you may be in the way.

Flatropers Wood *865 233,* ♀, *several paths, NR*

Flatropers is a nature reserve of the Sussex Naturalists' Trust – about a square mile, but adjoining other woods in one of those fascinating, remote country areas one is surprised to find in this century of sophisticated communications: cottages and farms amongst small irregular fields seemingly carved out of the woodland, and reached only by muddy lanes.

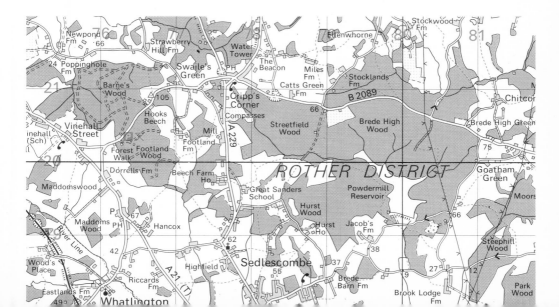

Bixley Wood and **Beckley Woods** are adjacent, the latter devoted to pines and Douglas fir but with a pleasant curving ride, littered with fungi in late summer and autumn – the commonest are Boletus species.

Flatropers is ancient, as its sculptured banks tell us at once. It contains good standard oaks, much birch – some trees quite large – and some chestnut coppice. The wood is kept tidy by hordes of large black wood ants, which sweep the litter into heaps of astonishing size and neatness. Beneath the heap the nest may extend a metre into the soil. The wood ants' pupal stage provides our goldfish with dried ants' eggs. Wood ants are said to milk aphids by artfully stroking them, and they attack caterpillars. They also are said to be noisy, rustling about the wood. This I did not notice, nor did I perceive any other form of wildlife; but I had a very nice *omelette aux girolles* for lunch.

There is a rustic crafts establishment near the turn off on the A268 – at a bend south of Four Oaks. There are no formal parking places for the woods.

Wood ants' nest in Flatropers Wood

Guestling Wood *864 146*, ♀, *26 acres, various easy walks, WT*
Attached to larger woods, privately owned, to the south, this is high Weald woodland with views over the River Brede.

Guestling Wood is managed largely by 'non-intervention', while some chestnut coppice is cut in rotation to preserve the traditional character. There is no formal parking place, and access is by the public footpath marked on the map or by other paths which cross the wood.

Hemstead Forest is large, 3 miles long, from north of Benenden to a mile short of Biddenden. The Forestry Commission car park, *813 344*, on a sunny Saturday morning seemed an entirely happy place: the larches on this high ground fit well enough into a landscape whose warm, clear colours and clean contours are familiar from calendar art, but not the less respectable. Traditional ways of caring for woods, orchards, hedges, fields, and houses have resulted in a scenery that anyone tired of haste and urbanization may find restores the spirit. The journey from London is short – very short considering that it takes you back a hundred years.

At Hemstead, ponies passed with Benenden girls, lovers met, and a few dogs got their fresh air; all seemed well with the world.

Angley Wood, *766 362*, west of Cranbrook, is a local nature reserve of the County Naturalists' Trust, for which you should have a permit.

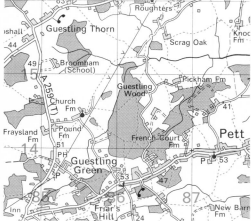

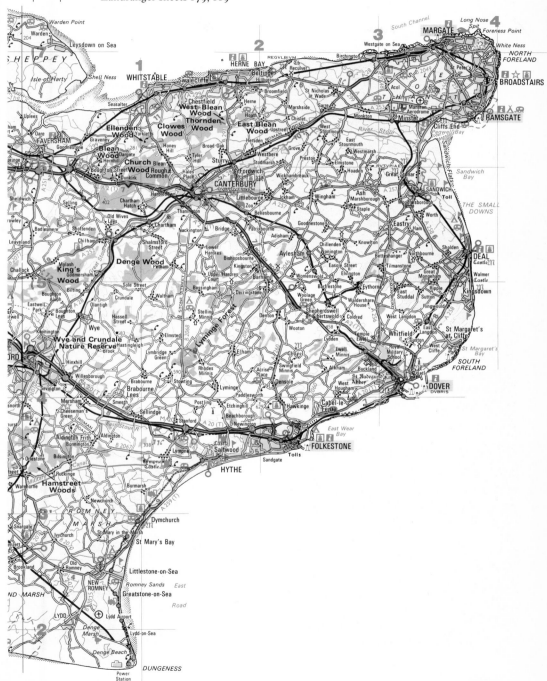

SCALE 1:316 800 or 5 MILES to 1 INCH

0 1 km = 0·6214 mile   5   10   Kilometres 15

0 1 mile = 1·61 kms   5   Miles 10

Hamstreet Wood *005 337*, ♀ , *40 acres, easy but damp, NR*

The Hamstreet Woods are all preserved, and accessible, even if they don't look so from the busy A2070. In Hamstreet turn down by the ugly Duke's Head to the new bungalows at Bourne Wood and left down the lane for the muddy Saxon Shore Way and the National Nature Reserve of 40 acres. The wood is quite charming, with an immediate wealth of native trees apparent, both species of oak and their hybrid being co-dominant, with ash, hornbeam, birch, aspen, sallow, guelder rose and even a wild service turning up as you go. The south side is hornbeam coppice and chestnut coppice: these are cut and used. It takes a little over an hour to walk all round the wood: take no notice of signs directing you to keep to the muddy bridleway: these are directed at horse riders. This reserve is only a

Hamstreet Wood: leaves of a wild service tree, with chestnut and hornbeam

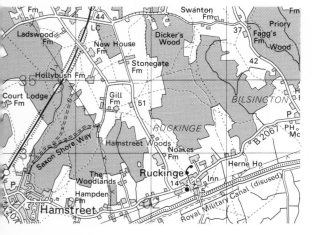

small part of 230 acres of woodland here, which are sensitively managed, using natural regeneration or local seed, and careful selection from old coppice stools, to produce good-quality hardwoods. Perhaps only in Kent, where people seem to be doing very largely what they always have, could such a compromise between nature and commerce be practised in this century. The warden has even found a market for hornbeam pulp wood; the trees are coppiced on a twenty-year cycle. We are told that you have to rise your voice to be heard above the nightingales on May evenings, and that three species of woodpecker have nested in the same tree, a dead oak left standing for that purpose.

Further west, more oakwood can be entered from the by-road parallel to the A2070, at *988 336*. Here you can see south over the marshes and the variety of species is less intense, nature less on its best behaviour. At the north corner of the by-road the Forestry Commission keeps its end up at **Faggs Wood**, *986 348*, with a pretty parking place and a walk through varied woodland around a small stream valley.

Clowes Wood *136 629*, ♀ , ♣ , *forest trail, FC and pf*

North and west of Canterbury is a great arc of woodlands known collectively as **Blean Woods**. Blean itself is a village on the Whitstable road with now only an indirect connection with the woodlands. A Forestry Commission picnic site, Clowes Wood, *136 629*, near the centre of the complex, provides a useful stopping place in a region of narrow but busy roads. From Canterbury take an un-numbered road to Tyler Hill. Alternatively, from Whitstable turn off the A299 at Chestfield Industrial Estate – the roundabout is marked by two large garages. Clowes Wood is not the most interesting section, but is welcoming in autumn with the heraldic reds and golds of the Forestry Commission's *Quercus rubra* and *Acer platanoides* which border the heavy blocks of spruce.

A quarter of a mile south of the Clowes Wood car park an even narrower road leads off through **Thornden Wood**, *145 634*, bordered by impenetrable chestnut coppice. Thornden

Wood is coniferized towards this, its western side, but there is still original sessile oak with chestnut understorey to the east where it is called, confusingly, West Blean Wood, a National Nature Reserve. It is bisected by a well-worn, decently surfaced public bridleway leading to Herne village.

East Blean Wood, *188 645*, by Herne Common, is 'private' and festooned with threatening yellow notices. The lane to Hoath goes through it and there are footpaths leading off, but absolutely nowhere to park. Enthusiastic walkers could park in Hoath and proceed westwards through East Blean, West Blean and Thornden Woods, crossing the A291 just north of the so-called Wealden Woodlands Wildlife Park – a commercial set-up – and possibly stopping at the popular Fox and Hounds which is on the route and does food. Emerging onto Thornden Wood Road, the narrow road mentioned above, you have an awkward two sides of a triangle of motor road before you reach the Clowes Wood car park. It is possible to cross the short side of the triangle but there is certainly no right of way at present. Since the alternative is uncomfortable and dangerous, I have written to the local authority to try to get a pathway across. A fine stand of black pine is now being clear-felled and the land replanted, so indiscriminate wandering is bound to be discouraged. It is sad that the tall pines must go; this must be a delectable place

on a fine day, and even on the very wet morning that I explored it I was irresistibly drawn to pause and sit on the damp bed of needles and gaze dreamily out at the greyness. Through Clowes Wood you can walk to the Red Lion, north of Blean on the A290, along a wide Forestry Commission bridleway, completing a 6-mile tramp from Hoath. Obviously, such a walk requires planning beyond the scope of this book, since without back-up transport there is no choice but to go back the same way. Less ambitiously, there is a labelled forest walk from the car park.

Blean Wood *075 608*, ♀, *pf*
Woods and commons to the south-west of Blean are quite accessible. Most attractive is Blean Wood – not 'West' or 'East' – near Dargate. Here you can park in Dargate and enter the wood by a path alongside an orchard, or, better, park at Holly Hill, *075 608*, just off a section of the old A2 between Dunkirk and Boughton Street. There is space for one or two cars where the well-marked bridleway crosses the road. Here is an unexpected atmosphere of moorland between the oakwoods – soft rush and hawthorn, with sheep grazing, and if your timing is right an efficient pair of sheep-dogs. At 300 feet above sea-level there is a good view to the north over Graveney Marshes to industrial Sheppey, yet with orchard land below you to prove you are not in Lancashire. To enter Blean Wood take the left fork to the

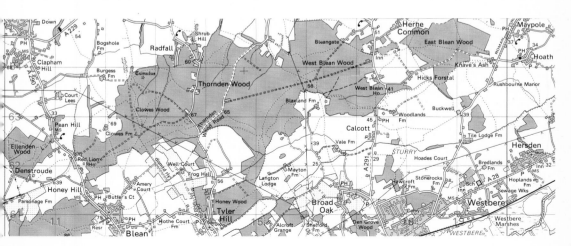

so-called Keeper's Cottage. Near the house there is a good deal of alien planting – even a silver fir or two. But keeping to the highest ground (a choice of several footpaths) you find yourself in pure oak coppice with bracken; on lower ground to the north is chestnut;

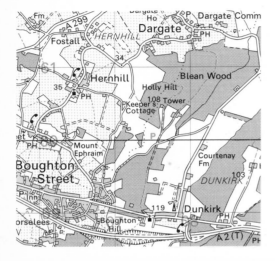

hornbeam towards Dargate. This is an excellent wood, full of interest and not spoiled by containing a few alien specimens. Wild service and aspen are present. South from Holly Hill you can easily walk in woodland by the small sawmill but you will soon reach the snarling A2(T). On the far side of this road are many woodlands between Winterbourne and Chartham Hatch; access via orchard roads and tracks is somewhat seasonal.

Denge Wood *113 525, ♀ , 64 acres, WT plus adjacent woodland*
Immediately south-west of Canterbury and south of the A28 lies the large Denge Wood – much larger than the 64 acres of it owned by the Woodland Trust; but this section provides access from Garlinge Green where one can park. The woods are old, with pollard hornbeams on ancient banks and some herbaceous plants associated with ancient woodland. The Trust will continue traditional management and will conserve a 14-acre patch of grassland in the middle of the wood.

Blean Wood

Between Blean Wood and Canterbury, 2 miles from the city, is a large area of rather tatty oak and chestnut woodland, **Church Wood**, invaded by birch and sycamore towards Rough Common, which is exactly what it says it is. Uneven ground, a breezy place to walk, with too many footpaths at the Rough Common end: more undisturbed where the bridleway reaches Denstroude Farm, *096 611*. Traditional split-chestnut palings or spiles were being made, using froe or dillaxe (side-cutting axe) with break (a vice with three-legged stand) under an awning in a coppice near the Dog and Punchbowl at Rough Common.

At Denstroude, north of these woods, is the smaller, thicker **Ellenden Wood**, *105 625*, a bird sanctuary of the Kent Naturalists' Trust. There is a bridleway from the Honey Hill road: but please don't take the dog. This oak and hornbeam wood used to contain wild service trees, but they were cut by mistake (for sycamore). Cow wheat grows under the trees, and the heath fritillary is found here. It feeds upon cow wheat and is local to Kent. Wood ants prey upon the caterpillars.

Lyminge Forest West Wood *141 440*, ✦, *FC*

From Canterbury the Roman road called Stone Street leads south straight as a plumb line – use it to reach the Forestry Commission's West Wood, near Mockbeggar. A bright blue-and-white garage marks the turning left: or first turn sharply right to buy untreated double cream at Lymbridge Green. Lyminge Forest West Wood has a most impressive car park used, of course, out of season, by no one except dog owners, at least one of whom does not even leave his car – the dogs know their route. The fine tall trees are mostly Douglas firs with some spruces; more workaday stands of timber lie beyond, including some beautiful young larches; dense, dark hemlock west of the car park. West Wood is quiet: only distant aeroplanes to be heard, and the occasional tearing noise as an unwanted native hardwood is uprooted.

Tall Douglas firs at Lyminge Forest West Wood

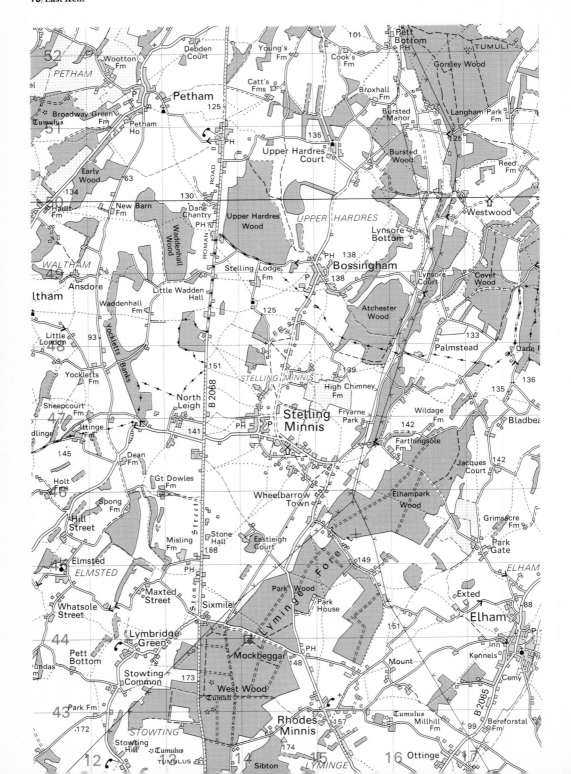

A DRIVE

Northwards from here through a long valley the lanes form a stretched-out network between patches of woodland separated by lonely, unfenced, arable fields, and with few settlements. The countryside is spectacular and unfrequented: a woodland walk by car if you like, with plenty of places to stop and explore. You could take a fortnight, and I didn't have a fortnight, unfortunately. This is all Lyminge Forest according to the Forestry Commission, and no doubt it is all in the process of change within limits imposed by timber production. The views are a little marred by high-tension pylons which follow the valley – but help one's sense of direction. From Pett Bottom, *161 521*, to Pett Bottom, *117 436*, is about 10 miles of some of the finest Kentish countryside, especially in its hedges, typical only of itself.

Dewy web in Challock Forest

conveniences. The prescribed walk sets off through chestnut coppice, first some years old, then recently cut with some standard hardwoods. The chestnut stools are, very refreshingly, fairly widely spaced, giving scope for exploration. Some are respectably ancient. I heard a fox bark in the distance, but on this wet, misty morning the visible wildlife was in the lovely forms of numerous spider-webs beaded with moisture, each exploiting exactly the fork of a chestnut twig but conforming to their species plan. After this overture the curtain rises on tall pinewood, very poetic, not dense, much chestnut remaining, and with tall bracken. The solemn arcades, full of mist, were impressive – as they must be in summer.

Sheltering in a hazel coppice, Crundale Downs

King's Wood, Challock *024 500*, ♀ ♣, *2½m, easy, FC*

Challock is the name of the third Forestry Commission complex in this section, and of the village about 5 miles north of Ashford. King's Wood is spread for 3 miles along the top of the North Downs and is about 2 miles wide. The cark park, *024 500*, is a short distance down the Wye road which forks from the A251 to Ashford less than a mile from Challock. (The village is pleasant, all new houses on a wide green with shop, garage, and pub advertising food.) The car park is just that, with no public

Wye and Crundale Downs *078 455*, ♀, *about 50 acres open, NNR*

Beyond the old town of Wye, taking the Hastingleigh road, you again climb to the top of the escarpment, this time to 550 feet, which when I went was well into the clouds. The nature reserve in the mist and rain appeared to have little to offer beyond a long row of very individualistic beeches. But, as I walked, the horizon became visible, and with it a strip of creamy light. Soon the sun had altered everything, and the cattle which graze the down began to emerge from a hazel thicket

where they had found some slight shelter.
Views over Kent and westward along the
Downs are inspiring, no less the rich textures
of grassland and scrubland below. The whole
nature reserve is 250 acres, and the small area
open to the public contains highly
characteristic woodland, from hazel coppice
with oak standards to pure coppice, and chalk
scrub, with spindle, wayfaring tree and
hawthorn. One hazel is unbelievably large,
bristling with hundreds of shoots. The coppice
is cut, but the wood, apparently, is left to rot,
the object being really to conserve the coppice
and keep dead wood as a habitat; no one needs
the fuel. The Visitors' Centre had some graphic
panels with facts about geology and wildlife,
but I felt it was out of place.

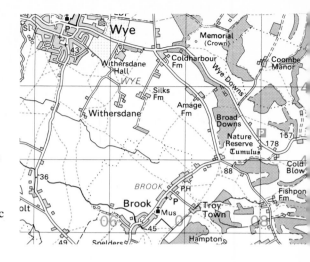

Looking south-east from Wye and Crundale Downs Nature Reserve

SOUTH-EAST ENGLAND
South Chilterns, Thames Downs, Surrey Heath Landranger sheets 164, 165, 174, 175

Reading is at the centre of this section, but the woodlands are mainly in the Chilterns to the north-west and the commons of the Bagshot Sands to the south-east. From the point of view of Londoners, great roads serve the area: the M40 bypassing High Wycombe; the M4 to Maidenhead; the M3 sweeping over Bagshot.

THE M40 TO THE CHILTERNS

Cowleaze Wood 726 957, ♀ ♣, 1m, easy, FC

Turning off the M40 at junction 5, to Stokenchurch, immediately turn left onto the old road, the A40(T), and left again, signposted Christmas Common. You now cross over the motorway as it plunges over the chalk and, incidentally, through Aston Rowant Nature Reserve – this in spite of fierce opposition in the 1950s. The Forestry Commission car park, large and among the trees, is invaluable, for there are no stopping places on Christmas Common roads. From the vicinity of the car park there is a wide view over Oxfordshire, the foreground framed by the ash, beech and oak of an old hedge. The view is enjoyed all the year round by a colony of gypsies in a by-road – who also manage to put up with some very cold winds. The waymarked walk leads back from the escarpment ridge through a larchwood and into a beechwood, then through spruces and out to a seemingly remote, enclosed countryside, patterned with hanging beechwoods and steep ploughland. The path along the south-east side of the wood is surprisingly well used, as if there were a secret traffic: perhaps lines of pack-horses winding along the wood margins in the dusk. There are maples, whitebeams, oaks.

On the eastern side of the motorway the A40 to Oxford sweeps in impressive curves down the escarpment through Aston Wood and Juniper Bank, both National Trust properties, not ideal walking country because of the road and the steepness. Woods to the north-east above Chinnor are also of mature beech,

Chiltern beechwood

By the side of Cowleaze Wood, Christmas Common

57

probably of natural origin, very beautiful, and somewhat spoiled by over-use and rubbish dumping.

South-west, near Christmas Common, is **Watlington Hill**, with two sections totalling 108 acres belonging to the National Trust and a car park at the top of the hill. South-

westwards on the high ground are well-shaped yews, like a township of green tents, for which the area is known. The path leads off from the car park along a line of shapely beeches. Most of the National Trust acreage is chalk escarpment, grassland with some scrub, levelling off to clay-with-flints above.

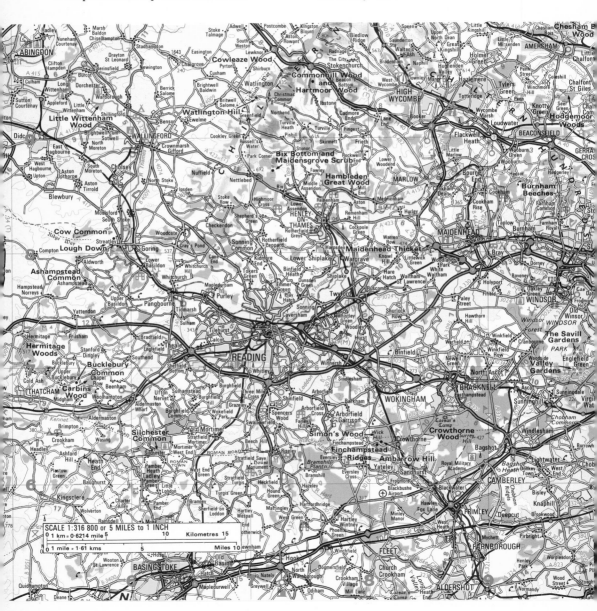

THE M4 BY MAIDENHEAD, THEN M423

Maidenhead Thicket *855 812, ♀ ♠, 364 acres, NT*
Just past the last roundabout of the motorway and miraculously intact is the Thicket, an appropriately triangular patch penetrated only by a muddy road. A popular place to park, but still very much a thicket, this is an old common with grazing long since discontinued. Thorns are old and picturesque; there are some old oaks, some beeches, and a stand of larch. Amongst the thorns a jungle is fast developing, but a wide grassy ride provides an easy walk with many attractive groupings of trees, returning (clockwise) by more open mature beeches and oaks surrounding Robin Hood's Arbour, an earthwork described in a notice-board on site. I have passed by Maidenhead Thicket many a time without realizing that it was more than a forgotten piece of scrub: it is in fact a woodland of some charm.

THE M40 OR THE M4

Burnham Beeches *956 852, ♀, 492 acres, many paths and roads, map on site, LA*
Turn north from the M4 junction 6 through Slough for Farnham, or south from the M40's junction 2 – a better route. The map reference applies to the large parking ground on East Burnham Common, a piece of open land, but you can drive in the woodland. Walking, the skill is to avoid the roads. I would suggest a circular, anticlockwise route taking in both streams to the north and then striking south to join the Victoria Drive. This route will take you through the characteristic, grotesque or beautiful to your taste, ancient pollard beeches for which the area is well known. Besides beeches, you will find gorse, broom, ling, rhododendron, oaks (some old pollards), birch, pine, sallow, holly, yew, brambles and bracken. The soil is not the chalk of the Chiltern beechwoods, but gravel of the river terraces.

Burnham Beeches is a sort of public park (since 1879) made out of what was effectively a common used without stint for grazing and firewood until, surrounded by coal-burning

houses, it passed simultaneously into disuse and into the affections of Londoners. Stoke Poges, with Thomas Gray's 'sentinel yews', is just to the south-east.

Hodgemoor Woods *960 940 and 968 938, ♀ ♠, 300 acres, 3 walks, easy, sometimes muddy, FC*
Surrounded by lanes as narrow as any in Devonshire – Bottom Lane around the south side and Bottom House Farm Lane leading off the north – this is a rich and highly characteristic patch of old woodland with a very busy birdlife. There are patches of young grand fir and Austrian pine, both looking extremely healthy, amongst oaks and birch coppice, with a few old Scots pines to establish a precedent for this coniferous invasion of a very picturesque wood. A few acres of oak have been cleared to plant beech, such are the mysteries of modern forestry. The car parks are pleasant with lots of grass, shade if needed. Three waymarked walks lead off: red $\frac{3}{4}$ mile, blue 1 mile, green $1\frac{1}{2}$ miles. Though not large this is a wood easy to get lost in, strangely mediaeval and directionless – so follow the markers.

Chesham Bois Wood *960 003, ♀, 40 acres, no particular routes, WT*
Bois is pronounced as Boys. This gloomy patch of close-set beeches is surrounded by houses and cut by a noisy road, and I cannot think

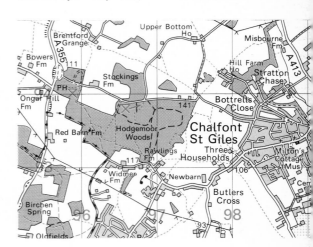

why the Woodland Trust bothered. Between the tracks of motorbikes, living dangerously, are scattered plants of woodruff and sanicle, some rather sad bluebells, gooseberry and much *Rubus*, not flowering. A clearing on the east slope has a magnificent display of grasses and rushes, a vigorous birch thicket coming up.

THE M4, M423, A423 TO HENLEY

Bix Bottom and Maidensgrove Scrubs
726 871, ♀ , 2m or more, steep, muddy in winter, NR
Bix, at the top of the hill out of Henley, on the A423(T) towards Nettlebed, is hard to miss. Turn into Bix village and follow the Lane to Little Bixbottom Farm and Valley End Farm. There is a wide grass verge to park on, or you can go as far as the nature reserve run by the Bucks, Berks and Oxfordshire Naturalists' Trust (BBONT). Here the Warburg Reserve is dedicated to conserving the maximum of

different habitat. There is a nature trail with a very clear booklet, and an exhibition open every day except Thursdays and Fridays.

For a plain walk with no lectures, follow the Oxfordshire Way path along the side of the valley, with a hedge of wayfaring trees, and into a wood called Freedom. At once you are in characteristic chalkland scrub with spurge laurel among fiercely armed trailing rose (*Rosa arvensis*) and many other chalk shrubs. Maple, ash and beech are growing, hardwoods planted since the wood was felled in 1954. At the top of the hill the path joins a rutted cart track and here you are clearly on clay. Besides the fact that it sticks to your feet, there is much more hazel. A very large blackthorn in winter was still covered with rotting sloes. The Scrubs are on the slope to your left and you will find a path downwards at the corner nearest Maidensgrove. This patch of weird woodland, mainly coppiced beech with hazel, is neither comfortable to walk in nor is it particularly

Old coppice trees in Hodgemoor Woods

interesting botanically, but I find it fascinating. At the foot of the hill you are at stage 1 of the nature trail: a large Christmas tree and a wide grassy ride, with rabbits, and, they say, in season, pyramidal, greater butterfly and common spotted orchids.

At this point you may decide to return by the road or follow the nature trail which circulates to the west. The Information Centre is a few yards back down the valley.

Driving in the complicated lanes of the Chilterns between Henley and the escarpment, one is hardly ever out of the cover of beeches. But often what appear to be walkable woods are quite narrow belts of trees, or, as at Nettlebed, so open that you never get away from motor noise. Near Checkendon you can park by a bridleway, *677 828*, which leads between Forestry Commission spruces with a wide and interesting band of native vegetation. You can also walk south-west through the open,

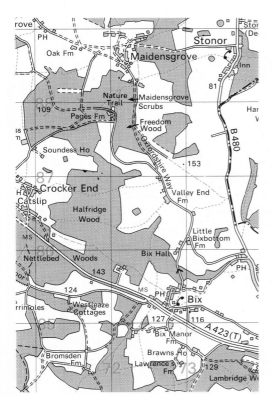

mature beeches of the Hook End Estate on bridleways and footpaths.

The lovely villages of Fingest and Turville at the centre of a still remote and still wooded dip-slope, are easily reached from Henley – take the A4155 Marlow road along the river, turning off to Hambleden. **Hambleden Great Wood**, and it *is* enormous, on a hogsback of chalk, is easily accessible by footpaths signed at the roadside. But you have to park in Hambleden itself and this can be difficult at holiday times. An official, not so convenient, parking place is at *785 856* north of Mill End.

Ibstone, *756 930*, more easily reached from the Stokenchurch junction (5) of the M40 (turn away from Stokenchurch at the exit lane) has open beechwoods, very beautifully shaped and at the right density, with some oak and holly – **Commonhill Wood** and **Hartmoor Wood**, *750 950*. Ibstone Common itself has an interesting corner of scrub again leading by well-marked footpaths into beechwoods. This almost brings you back to Christmas Common. Long-distance walkers may follow the Oxford-shire Way through and beside beechwoods and over Christmas Common. The area thus described is small but it is difficult to get to know and on ordinary weekdays very quiet indeed.

Oxford University Arboretum, Nuneham Courtenay *555 987, 45 acres, very easy, pf*

The arboretum is 5 miles south of Oxford on the A423, a Victorian collection of conifers, Japanese maples, etc, to which new trees of special botanical or economic interest have been added. A rare patch of Greensand allows the cultivation of calcifuges. (The alluvial terraces of the Thames are mostly limy.) The plantation is informal and resembles woodland, with peacocks as a change from the usual game.

The arboretum is open only between April and September and is closed on Sundays.

NEAR ABINGDON

Little Wittenham Wood *566 934, ♀ (♠), 180 acres, bridleway and footpath, muddy, pf*

The Thames or Isis meanders around Long Wittenham (which has an island with a rare

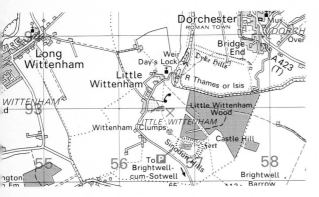

nor did Mrs Buntsey's Buttocks (after a local landowner). On the river side are poplars, on the hill side spruces; in between, where the bridleway waits to trap you in mire, is Oxfordshire oak/ash woodland, and very nice too.

You can walk up to the Clumps, which are of beech, and admire the distant Downs, the nearer Didcot Power Station and nearer still Dorchester Meres. From Little Wittenham northwards a line of not very successful, but attractive, fastigiate poplars leads your eye along a forgotten road over the flat land to the site of a lost village – 'lost' little over a century ago.

THE M4 BY READING (Junction 12)

What you might call the Pangbourne Downs is a rectangle enclosed on two sides by major roads, on the east by the Goring-Pangbourne Gorge or Gap in the Downs and, for our purposes, by the Ridge Way crossing south of Blewbury. Yattendon, Hampstead Norreys and Ashampstead are lovely quiet places in softly moulded valleys of the Downs, patched with woodland and stitched with many footpaths. No walk can be entirely woodland here, but that is part of the magic; the sudden views of well-shaped hills and noble groups of farmsteads, the houses of brick and tile, with nice old barns.

wood of pollard willows) and Little Wittenham, where it was forded by the Romans from Silchester, who paused here to graze their beasts. A little below, the Thames is joined by the much less formidable Thame. Dorchester, with its once very important Abbey, is on the Thame. A favourite walk leads from Dorchester over the meadows and a large double dike to the weir bridge at Day's Lock and Little Wittenham church close by.

At Little Wittenham church, tiny and dwarfed by great *Sequoiadendron* in a garden, you walk across a field to Little Wittenham Wood. The wood is between the river and the shade side of the double Sinodun Hills or Wittenham Clumps. Wittenham Dugs, the local name since the mounds were furnished with these clumps, did not get onto the map,

Ashampstead Common *578 754, ♀ ♣, 200 acres, bridleway, muddy, common land*
Any common is a draw to the walker, particularly in our case if it is wooded, and this one is wooded with a vengeance. Do not attempt to park on the road which runs through the middle. The map reference gives a north-west corner where there is space by a cottage and a glimpse of the chalky down; the common is on clay-with-flints. You can also park at the other side of the wood.

It appears that the common was originally an oak-and-beech wood with holly, yew, hawthorn and some cherry. It is overgrown: Scots and Weymouth pines and Douglas firs are now taller than the oaks and there are weirdly shaped beeches, birches, thorns and hollies grown up from old coppice; moss everywhere, thickets of oak and beech saplings. It is a fairytale wood perhaps; it must have looked a Cinderella wood when all the timber oaks were removed, probably in the 1914–18 war, leaving nothing but misshapen beeches and frowsty thorns. The Prince, in the person of the Lord of the Manor, came and planted exotic conifers; and Princess Cinderella is now left to decay in her finery. It is a long time obviously since anyone exercised any common rights here; you would think they would at least gather up the dead wood. It is a shame, and nothing like a common, but it is worth seeing and if the sun shines you will be rewarded with an aged smile.

There are other commons like this – Holme Wood near Dorking is one – I suppose no one dares to touch them.

South of the M4 – no barrier but a blessed pipeline bleeding off the noise from this nice countryside – and under it, you come to beautiful Bradfield, Southend, Scotland and Bucklebury Common, on which last there is a parking place which wins my prize for decency: no rubbish, a sensible litter bin, no sequestering trees, heath of gorse and birch. A shallow screen of sallows is planted. Cars zoom by as if trying to reach take-off speed, but you can't have everything.

Carbins Wood, Bucklebury Common
561 693, ♀ ♣, 600 acres, easy but muddy, ½–3m, FC and common land

The common is lined with houses lurking behind the steep, old wood-bank which separates heath from woodland; the gnarled oaks on the bank are glimpsed beyond the birch and the gorse. Between a house rather confusingly called Carbins Wood and a used car lot of distinctly woodland type, you can progress down to a stream and the pretty edges of the Forestry Commission wood. There are stands of beech and larch, with pines and Douglas firs, all nicely varied. The path along the stream, lined with elegant silver birches, is most attractive, with the plantation shutting off the noise and wind, and a hint or two of old coppice to remind us that the wood is old. Bluebells push vigorously through the dry leaf litter of the beeches.

If you take the direct path southwards on a grassy ride you soon reach the south margins of the wood – another stream and a paddock

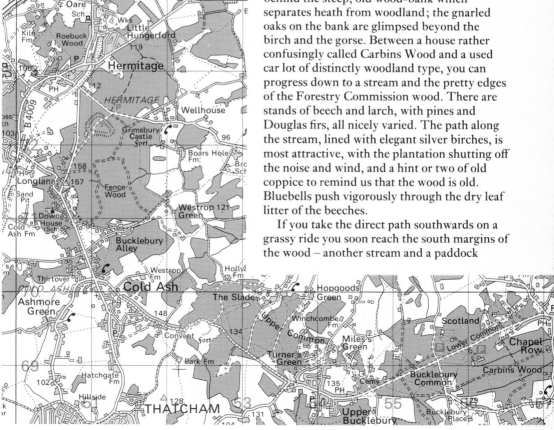

Path by the stream in Carbins Wood

surrounded by oaks and cherries of some age. Of course, Carbins must have been an oakwood, perhaps with beech on this more fertile side. Perhaps the drama of the place, besides its attractive uneven ground, is the contrast between birch heath and oakwood, in spite of the new planting. Anyway, I thought it was all quite charming, partly of course because of the weather, which was my favourite combination of low sunlight against darkening clouds in the east. How the birch trunks and gorse flowers gleamed in that light! The large cherries will be splendid in early May, so will the bluebells, perhaps earlier.

Bucklebury Common continues to Upper Common, with pines adding a darker note westwards towards Cold Ash. The Slade, at the north-west, is a heavily wooded part – oak and beech – which I was pleased to see was being cut and harvested. The tractors churn the ground, but there is a path along the edge which looked promising, starting at *523 695*, at the Convent – or the road itself is quiet enough. A slade is a wet hillside.

Pangbourne itself has, it seems, little to offer away from the attractive but often busy riverside; but some trains from Oxford or Reading do stop there, and one might take a bicycle to ride the straightish lane westwards onto the Downs; about 5 miles to Ashampstead. Basildon Park, National Trust, is architecturally imposing but boring parkwise, with ugly limes in front and a dull beech plantation marked private. The great arboretum of the area is **Cliveden**, near Taplow, *915 840*, open seasonally, National Trust; the heavily wooded Cliveden reach of the river is often pictured. There are seventeenth-century yew hedges, ancient mulberries, great glades of *Ilex*, cypress oaks, butternut trees, and *Rhododendron macabeanum*. Nearby the lamented **Dropmore**, with many great trees, is now secured behind tall wire fences, with absentee Arabian owners and resident Alsatian defenders.

Lough Down, Streatley *583 806*, ♀ *(scrub)*, *28½ acres, ½m, short grass, hilly, NT*
On the B4009 just out of Streatley there is a

rather abysmal parking place, once elm shaded; but over the stile you are in a world away from, and above, mere motor cars. The wood at your right is not interesting except as a foil to the lovely view, the foreground occupied by well-controlled scrub on the grass slope. The hedge (golf on the far side) is also nice. This is a short, non-woodland walk, well worth seeking out on a fine day. The wood has a path along the side, and there is another piece of National Trust downland on the other side of Streatley.

More chalk scrub is visible from the Ridge Way, which climbs to its proper altitude through a dry valley west-north-west of Streatley. Take the first turning left north of the village, marked (always a good sign) 'No Through Road, Golf Club'. At Warren Farm a notice informs you of the civilized compromise that has been reached between rough riders and walkers on this path: in short, don't ride on Sundays and holidays. If you are worried about the springs and clearance of your car don't drive. The walk to the woods is only one slow mile between sycamores.

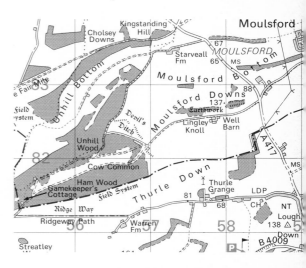

Cow Common, Unhill Wood, Ham Wood *551 813*, ♀ ♣ , *about 500 acres, up to 3m, easy, pf and now a NR*
From the Ridge Way you enter the woods by the Gamekeeper's Cottage to a chorus of loud assorted dog music, and if you have a dog it

really must be on a lead. The gamekeeper is cheerful and informative.

The shapes of the woods are fascinating around the serpentine, undulating Cow Common – not common any more and without cows but with a variety of gamebirds. In winter the dark branches and green trunks of the beeches contrast vividly with the chalky soil and the bleached grass, and some not-too-oppressive spruces and Douglas firs add their own colours, seemingly a brighter green here on the chalk. The distant Downs are blue. There is a not-very-old wood-bank (say 250 years) alongside the path covered in moss, dog's mercury and bluebells. Many beeches here did not survive the drought a few years back, and there is also a slight plantation effect of even-age and cherry laurel, but these are very beautiful woods, partly coniferized but with much evidence of old use. Large cherries have been allowed to get too old and rotten and little serious forestry is practised: shooting was the purpose of the woods, now a nature reserve of the BBONT. You can enter from the other direction, by Starveall Farm from the A417, striking up from Unhill Bottom.

Blewbury, home of Ratty and Mole, has amongst other things (notably thatched walls) a wood in its middle and a little stream. The trees are very tall and I do not know what will happen when they have to come down.

SOUTH OF THE M4 AND THE A4

Burghfield Common is a village on a Hampshire bit of the Surrey Heath district and as its name suggests has much common land – poor sandy heath with birches and colonizing Scots pines. The inhabitants treat the common as if it were an old doormat, which it resembles in places. There are some plantations of pine, and the various stages of gorse, birch and pine are interesting away from the tatty edges. When Amey Roadstone have finished with their quarries and greened them over the whole area might be turned into a valuable recreation zone. Towards Mortimer Station – Blowers Common – the ground is uneven with old quarry holes. Towards Mortimer West End there are more oaks than beeches, some signs

of old woodland, and even a notice saying 'no unauthorized motorcycling'.

Some of the pine stands are tall and make impressive woods. There is something rather touching in the way this tree has returned to a prehistoric home – though of course these are descendants from a European, not a native, strain of *Pinus sylvestris*.

Aldermaston Soke has spruce and a timber industry to the north, and fine open pinewood to the south near Silchester. Silchester Roman town, *Calleva*, preserves, because never built over, the original plan, where were found many sub-fossil seeds of fruit trees, altering our views about Roman tree introductions – but not conclusively, for the Romans were great importers of favourite foods. There is a museum in the village.

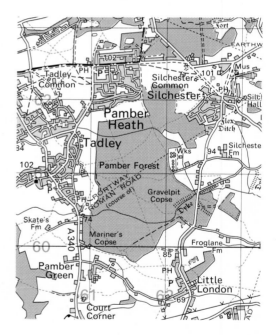

Silchester Common, Pamber Forest
627 623, ♀ ♠ ♨, 1½ hours at least, very wet in places, common land and NR
There is ample parking by the sports ground, prettily surrounded by shining gorse in summer. This gorse common should be treated with respect: its northern segment is peaty and trackless; beware, however innocent it may

look. Keep on high ground or you may be trapped like a fly in a bottle.

Walk down the road signed to Lords Wood and the Butts, a new housing estate. An old wooden sign points to the footpath, which skirts the backs of the new houses and soon leaves the gorse-and-birch heath for oak woodland. At the bottom, signs lead you left into Pamber Forest and Nature Reserve. This is a fine wood of durmast oak giving way gradually to an equally fine stand of pine, now probably ready for thinning. Turn right at the crossways to descend to a charming stream through oak and hazel coppice, the banks mossy and strewn with common wild flowers – much wood anemone. Continuing, you will meet the prominent double wood-bank at the north side with gnarled oaks of ancient hedges, gorse beyond but all sylvan within. Return to meet the stream again – and this is important – follow it to rejoin the footpath. Any attempt to cross the common in what seems the right direction will lead you into the mire, with houses visible all round but no way out except

back. For a longer walk turn left and south at the crossways mentioned above; you will then cross the track of a Roman road more or less at right angles.

THE A30 TO STAINES

Virginia Water: the Savill Gardens *977 705* and **Valley Gardens** *984 700, ♀ ♣, easy, Crown Estate*
The Savill Gardens, created in 1932, are 35 acres, entrance quite costly, open from March to Christmas Eve, 10–6 (or 7 pm in summer). There is a bookshop and a café. The Valley Gardens, created in 1947, are 300 acres, free and open all the year.

Parking in this part of Windsor Great Park is not free and a supply of ten-pence coins is necessary – unless you pay to walk in the Savill Gardens, when a parking token is issued. From the strict point of view of woodland, the Valley Gardens offer more acreage, obviously, but for the maximum interest in an out-of-season, short walk the Savill Gardens are hard to beat.

Pamber Forest: a stand of pines

A great Scots pine by Virginia Water

The gardens are dominated by a small hill with tall beeches, the floor intriguingly covered with moss, looking like a vast collection of Victorian pincushions. This moss is not a mere gardeners' conceit for it grows elsewhere in Windsor Great Park. Everywhere on lower ground in March is a host of golden *Narcissus cyclamineus*, as pretty a flower as can be seen at any season anywhere, and there are drifts of crocuses under poplars and maples. North-west is a stand of *Tsuga heterophylla*, the western hemlock, underplanted with some of the weird and wonderful rhododendrons which are a feature of the place: *Rhododendron macabeanum*, for instance, is a spreading, angular tree with massive features: thick twigs, enormous leaves and custard-cream-coloured

flowers which in bud are like wizened clenched fists. I cannot normally tolerate rhododendrons, dark dusty green for most of the year and mostly the tree weed *R. ponticum*, but characterful species like these Tibetan giants soon win me over. The rhododendron much in bloom in March was 'Praecox', but hidden in the shrubbery 'Golden Oriole' was splendid. Camellias are strong here: *Camellia japonica* 'Gloire de Nantes' was still glorious in early March.

A fine Weymouth pine had scattered its open cones over what looked like quite ordinary daffodils. Such effects of random beauty are found only in the untouched wilderness or in well-cared-for gardens. Piles of what looked like discarded tramps' coats by the lake are the great leaves of *Gunnera*, left to keep the dormant plant warm. There are some very old English oaks in and around the garden; this is, after all, Windsor Great Park.

At Valley Gardens there is more walking to be done and the effects are broader. Also there is a wide range of pinetum species including *Tsuga* and a grove of *Metasequoia*; amazing great cedars and big Scots pine. But for a feast of colour when English woods are grey, the Savill Gardens are good value. The café is unpretentious and pleasant and overlooks the gardens. The car park proves to be surprisingly entertaining, with visits from pied wagtails, a jay and a crowd of lesser birds including chaffinches.

The more typical oak parkland is to be found at the western side of Windsor Great Park.

Savill Gardens' early specialities: *Narcissus cyclamineus* and *Rhododendron* 'Praecox'

M3 TO BAGSHOT

Ambarrow Hill, Finchampstead Ridges, Simon's Wood *813 635,* ♀ ♣
(Scots pine), 1¾m one way, easy but uneven, NT

At Finchampstead, Little Sandhurst, there is a complex of woodland around an avenue of large and impressive *Sequoiadendron giganteum*, the Big Tree of the Sierra Nevada, northern California, and the oldest and biggest tree in the world. Introduced to Britain in 1853 the tree was named after the Duke of Wellington, an indication of the importance of the Duke, but a name not acceptable to Americans who mostly call it the giant sequoia or Sierra redwood. Even Sequoia, after a Cherokee Indian chief, is hardly appropriate, for the Cherokees were forcibly evacuated from their Plains, far away from the High Sierra. Anyway, Wellington College is close by, beyond Crowthorne Station, and here are the wellingtonias, unfortunately bordering a motor road and forming an over-dramatic setting for the comings and goings of tradesmen's vans and schoolchildren.

Ambarrow Hill is crowned with tall Scots pines, the ground eroded by many pairs of shoes. The footpath will lead you to Ambarrow Lane, past the gardens of large houses and a field, to Finchampstead Ridges, where a sample of the beautiful Surrey Heath countryside of bracken, heather, birch and pine is preserved, overlooking the Blackwater River. Simon's Wood contains a large National Trust parking place and here of course this heathland walk might best start: but you can park at the roadside also.

Crowthorne Wood (Caesar's Camp)
862 661, (♀)♣, an easy stroll, or a tough hike needing boots and compass

Caesar's Camp, as usual with such names, is not Roman but pre-Roman, the third largest hill fort in Berkshire, with mighty ramparts now clothed in beech. That such a large structure should have been made here is a reflection on the native vegetation, which cannot have been all forest: it may have been grazing land. The site has not been excavated but it has been much trampled over. The Forestry Commission runs a wayfaring course into the coniferized Crowthorne Wood (information from Bracknell Sports Centre). Paths and rides are many and complex and the wood is large. The car park, rather cramped, is opposite a notice indicating Caesar's Camp on

Ambarrow Hill

Pattern of forestry in the Hermitage Woods

Nine Mile drive, which is off the A322 (Bagshot to Bracknell section). The turning is difficult to see, at a corner on a slight rise. Off the A3095 is a Forestry Commission picnic place in the (again) coniferized Edgebarrow Wood, *840 625*, just north of Sandhurst.

NEAR NEWBURY

Hermitage Woods *513 724,* ♀ ♣ *, 400 acres plus, easy, wet, pf*
Hermitage is a suburb, clearly indicated from Newbury's ring road and from the A34(T), and it has some really charming woodland where one can walk at will, only observing the sign-written admonishment of the owners, the Gerald Palmer Trust, to 'behave quietly'. I explored the northern segment of Fence Wood, and was very struck by the intimate and varied quality of mixed woodland clearly exploited for timber yet losing nothing – in fact gaining – in character. Larches were in the pretty fresh green they wear in April, beeches were in leaf already, oaks were impressive in

adolescent crowds or decorous in old age. A cuckoo rehearsed its notes and a deer paused in a patch of sunlight. A fine baby owl, fallen from its nest, was spotted by a pair of boxers and hurried off to Newbury by the boxers' owners: I'm sure it will return to its Hermitage. All was well with this little world. Everyone behaved quietly.

See the map on page 63.

20	21	22
17	**18**	19
13	14	15

SOUTH-EAST ENGLAND
London Woodland

Landranger sheets 176, 177, 187, 188

NORTH AND WEST LONDON

Hampstead Heath: Ken Wood *268 874, ♀, easy but not flat, 1m, LA*

The nearest wood to the middle of London is Ken Wood, about 30 acres, 4 miles as the starling flies from Trafalgar Square. Kenwood House is an important picture gallery and museum, the Iveagh Bequest; its gardens and wood are joined with but distinct from Hampstead Heath as a whole, like a vital organ within a living body. The wood is said to be a remnant of the Middlesex Forest – if so it is probably the only remnant – and is carefully fenced off. All the paths are fenced too, for this is a wood where the visitors annually much outnumber the trees. Oak, beech and chestnut are tall, and as classical in character as the music which on some summer evenings floats, curiously fragmented, from a concrete shell at the lakeside. There are good specimen trees in the garden, including a tall swamp cypress by the water's edge.

The car park nearer to Spaniards Gate best serves the woods. Close at hand, passing by a large (alien of course) horse-chestnut literally surrounded by small balsam, is North Wood, where English oaks and prolific undergrowth give an immediate impression of forest wilderness in spite of invading sycamore. Bear left by the terrace and the lake for Ken Wood itself.

Around Ken Wood to Parliament Hill

Taking a right-hand path out of the parking ground brings you to an open field, planted with red oak, scarlet oak, copper beech, well-shaped sweet chestnuts, and at the far right a great turkey oak – a family group, for all are Fagaceae. Further on is the wet western corner

Hampstead Heath Extension in winter – old hawthorn hedge

of Ken Wood with birches, hornbeams and rushes. Beyond this you may climb to an interesting pine-clad hill and then to the south-east side of Ken Wood: heathy, with birches. There are too many paths of course, but this is a quiet, strangely wild-feeling hillside to be so close to the middle of a large city. To the south is Parliament Hill, not without its woodland edges, and beyond is Gospel Oak, named after a boundary tree long disappeared. (Passages from the Gospel were recited to bless the bounds in Rogation Week.)

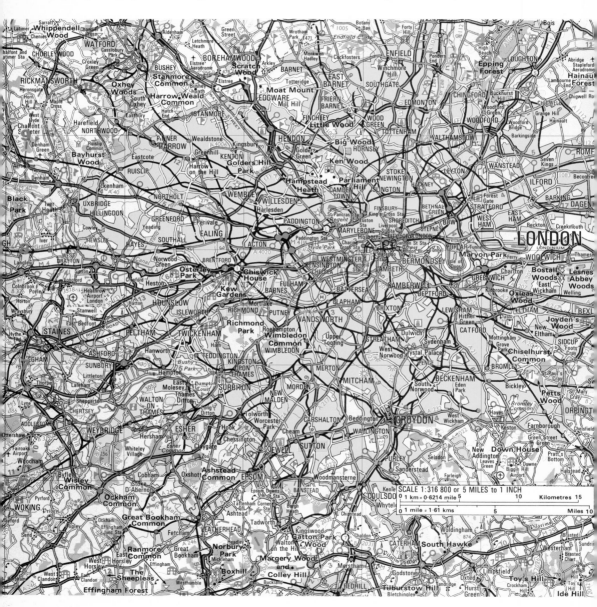

A Hampstead Heath Walk *about 2½m, can be muddy*

Ken Wood is best reached by car or bus, avoiding holidays and fine Sundays in summer, or it could be the focus of a longer walk. But for the best of Hampstead's woodland, take a number 24 bus to South End; or there is a large car park here at *271 859*, sheltered by fine weeping willows on East Heath Road. Hampstead Tube Station is not the best way to the Heath. From South End Road head towards the ponds, which are surrounded by large crack willows. Keep to the lowest ground, following the valley until you can cross to the far side, where you will find a wide path which eventually goes by a viaduct over a small, dark lake. There are many oldish oaks of character-istic shape, and silver birches, as well as a great richness of sallows and some alder. The grey squirrels are tame enough to eat out of your hand, if you have something they like. Climbing up towards Spaniards Way you enter a planted area with maples, Swedish whitebeam and, left towards the road junction at the top of Hampstead Heath, a number of false acacias (*Robinia*) which are naturalized in the sandy soil. You may now either cross Spaniards Road for the Hampstead Heath Extension or go left towards Jack Straw's Castle for Hill Gardens, West Heath and Golders Hill Park.

Option one takes you downhill through genuine secondary woodland. The land was quarried for sand and gravel until compara-tively recently. Birch has spread over the broken ground, especially to the south side, and there are ponds and even mires. Bur-marigold and Himalayan balsam are common here. In the steep woodland section to the right or north are naturally regenerating *Robinia* and Norway maple among a good mixture of native species including birch and oak, and with even a tall crab apple. The short descent brings you to the **Hampstead Heath Extension** which penetrates into the Hampstead Garden Suburb. This section of the heath is surrounded by a road with quasi-Georgian houses and plane trees, but you may strike through the centre of the grassland among oaks and overgrown hawthorn hedges (splendid in May) and still think yourself in the country.

Wildwood Road, on the east side, has many interesting planted specimens: hornbeam at the wood end, a *Paulownia* in a garden next to a *Catalpa* in the road (or it may be the other way around), still some surviving hedgerow oaks, and a planted wild service of excellent shape and unfailing fruit. You may cross the grass to find your way easily through the streets to Golders Green Station.

For option two, walk left along Spaniards Way until you can enter the woods, here a mixture of trees, including beech, sycamore and hybrid lime, surrounding a patch of open grass, all of which suggest the site of a former garden. The limes sucker exuberantly in the manner of this hybrid, but seedlings also are to be found in some years. In the grass are

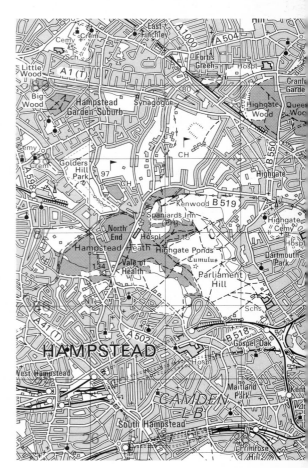

coltsfoot and yarrow, plants of bare or disturbed ground, though the disturbance must have been some time ago here.

Cross North End Road with Jack Straw's Castle on your left. This timber-clad landmark is a useful pub, with bar food. The damp path, between steep banks covered with sycamore suckers and seedlings, leads to West Heath, which is heavily wooded; or, more interestingly, you can climb some iron steps to surface through cherry laurel onto a stone parapet or walk-way. From this you can look down on a very fine hornbeam, while on your right are the serene lawns and cedars of Inverforth House. A great *Wisteria sinensis* clasps a column and spreads over a timber

Golders Hill Park in spring – Japanese cherries

pergola in a mildly extravagant architectural finish to this agreeable aerial promenade. You descend, almost through the branches of an old, wandering chestnut, to Hill Garden, as peaceful a place as can be found in London. Even here there is an aspect of woodland in a sheltering bank which supports beech trees which have enormous straight trunks. Beyond is **Golders Hill Park**, *258 877*, with deer and other animals in enclosures and many interesting trees. North-west (in springtime) there is a splendid collection of flowering cherries and pears. If it is autumn you will find a few fruits, probably, and easily pick out the dusky pink of *Cercis siliquastrum*, the Judas tree. To your left on the west side of the park, beyond the deer enclosure, is a wilder-looking section near the stream: not really wild, for you will find a beautiful cut-leaved alder (the variety 'Imperialis' of the common alder), a *Catalpa* and some tortuous willows – a now popular cultivar of a rare Chinese willow, *Salix matsudana*. But some very large hawthorns must have been there before all the planting. If you go out by the tennis courts, Golders Green Station is only a street away. If you have children allow at least an hour for looking at the animals.

Big Wood *254 886*, ♀, *18 acres, very easy paths with seats, LA*
Amazingly preserved, almost pickled in ripe suburbia, this is an oak-hazel wood, obviously an old coppice with standards. It is well worth seeking out (make for Temple Fortune Hill). The oaks are carefully looked after, no dead wood being allowed, probably for the safety of those who walk here. The large trees allow enough light for the hazel below to flower and there is a shrub layer of bramble in parts. For Londoners unreasonably missing the country in January, Big Wood is reassuring and delightful. Undoubtedly the isolation and seclusion of this small wood amongst acres of quiet streets and gardens allow it to function as a real wood and as a true bird sanctuary – not just a museum-piece bathed in petrol and diesel fumes. Grey squirrels are many but seem to do no harm.

Big Wood is only big compared with **Little Wood**, 2 acres, 200 yards to the north-west.

Beyond are the horrors of the North Circular Road, now without even its Cornish or Wheatley elms. Even so, crossing that road will bring you to a charming wooded park at Church End, *251 905*, with fine Caucasian wingnut, *Ginkgo*, Bhutan pine, etc, and a rare, cut-leaved oak by the pond.

Moat Mount *211 941*, ♀, ¼*m, fps, LA*
Another 4 miles outwards, and you are at the edge of the main sprawl of the Great Wen, where patches of open land still occur between satellites such as Edgware, Barnet and Borehamwood, the last a wood in name only. Between these is a large scheduled open space with a wood, Moat Mount. The entrance,

1 mile north of the junction called Northway Circus on the A1(T) or Barnet Way, is reached by going on to the next roundabout – another mile – and returning on the south-bound carriageway. There is parking only in a lay-by. This wood, which has survived from domestic parkland, is beautiful in spite of institutional trappings, and most remarkable for its hornbeams, once pollarded and now giving just a hint of old London woodland. By the lake (artificial and uphill) are *Quercus ilex* and other park trees.

On the opposite side of the A1 is a golf links and north of it Thistle Wood, Boys Hill Wood and Scratch Wood, now overlooking the service station called Scratchwood on the M1.

Hornbeams at Moat Mount

A link road is planned, and this area is likely to become a dumping ground, or a planned desert, but the woods are still accessible from another lay-by on the A1(T). Noise is an element here, above the motorway.

Whippendell Wood, Watford *073 978,* ♀ (♣), *200 acres, many dry fps, LA*

Watford, $16\frac{1}{2}$ miles from London, and only 15 minutes from London on the M1, could be described, much to its surprise, as the gateway to the Hertfordshire countryside. At the north end of the High Street is Cassiobury Park, and you can walk through this old and grand, but now sad, parkland, across the Grand Union Canal and the golf links, to Whippendell

HORNBEAM, Carpinus betulus

The coppices and the Loughton pollards were for fuel; it is'nt a craftsman's wood. Almost too hard and quite heavy, it was good for pulleys and screws, but you can make a better mallet, say, from elm, unsplittable, and ash, tough but resilient as well. Where hornbeam grows other trees are available, and bits of elm went from Buckinghamshire to replace mill-cogs in hornbeam-rich Hertfordshire.

You may still see it pleached and cut into ornamental hedges, a formal garden tradition sometimes translated to woods where strong hedges were needed – this gives a spurious distribution.

A much used and knocked-about tree, it can be large and fine. There must have been forests of it once, shady as beechwoods. A vigorous fastigiate form, neat and fan-shaped, is now planted as a street tree.

Wood. By car the more attractive of two car parks is approached by a single-track road from the Clarendon Arms at Chandler's Cross (signpost to the wood).

Though lately circumscribed by the link road A405(T), Whippendell Wood still has an aura of wildness, seeming to absorb the westerly winds and turning its back on industrial Watford. The fields around are very green. Older trees are beeches, their days numbered, and there are many oaks with burred trunks, reassuringly native. The field layer is intermittent bramble and bracken; there are birches of various ages, with holly a frequent shrub. There is a patch of Forestry Commission spruce to the north. Hedge trees are cut as coppice, decorative without being useful, and beech saplings, distinct with red leaves in midwinter, show that, catastrophe avoided, Whippendell Wood will survive.

RUISLIP AND NORTHOLT

Bayhurst Wood *070 891,* ♀ , *moderate, many routes, LA*

The car park is in the outermost westerly wood of a group of oakwoods, in total about 700 acres, around Ruislip Common. Across the lane is Mad Bess Wood, while Copse Wood and Park Wood are on each side of the Common, which is on the far side of the A4180. Turn off the A4180 opposite Ruislip Lido down Breakespeare Road, then right at Fine Bush Lane, for Bayhurst Wood. Ruislip is at the edge of the conurbation, its fields typically punctuated by kennels, small industries, farmhouses rebuilt in ranch style; but the woods are something like the original vegetation of the London Clay. **Oxhey Woods**, 2 miles north-east of Bayhurst Wood on the A4125, are also of native oak, even more public and accessible, but surprisingly wild in appearance for their suburban status. Many a front garden in the streets round about contains an oak of undoubted native origin, so that Ruislip and Northolt are rich in woodland atmosphere. The woods are Public Open Spaces – a sort of wood-pasture for people. As the trees approach maturity, conservation will have to take more aggressive forms.

Interestingly wet, **Stanmore Common,** *161 946,* is a small wood hemmed in by a large factory and a large hospital. It may be useful for local horse riders but is not specially attractive to walk in. Oakwood also survives at **Harrow Weald Common,** *143 926,* with a section of Grim's Dyke, and a viewpoint over Harrow Weald Park.

WEST FROM LONDON

Black Park *004 833,* ♠ *(♀), about 300 acres, very easy, can be wet, LA*
Not quite as far and not anywhere near as seductive as Burnham Beeches is Black Park, easily reached from London by the A40: turn on to the A412 at the final roundabout where the M40 begins. Black Park is on the right 3 miles on. It really is black, with lovely tall *Pinus nigra* and a lake surrounded by black mud – and very important-looking notices such as 'NO FISHING AFTER 5 P.M.'. There are beeches, silver birches and Scots pines as well, and a patch of pole conifers. Pinewood Studios is to the north. There is a map at the parking place with a suggested walk which takes in the new plantation. Just here and there, and even on the dullest day, there is a hint of a countryside quite unexpected for outer London and even Britain. Black Park is well loved by those who live round about, and it is close at hand for Uxbridge, which is otherwise hemmed in by aerodromes and reservoirs – though with a possible escape for walkers by the Grand Union Canal to Denham.

Black pine, beech and silver birch in Black Park

NORTH-EAST LONDON

Epping Forest *411 983 (High Beach),* ♀, *6000 acres including 2000 acres of grassland, GLC*
The trees of the forest cover an area about 6 miles long and nowhere more than $1\frac{1}{2}$ miles wide. For most of its length the forest is bisected by the A104, and is like a long, uneven oak leaf veined by roads and streams. There is a close network of paths and rides, but only one formal parking place, at High Beach, and cars are kept strictly to the roads.

Epping Forest occupies a broad ridge of gravel between the Lee and the Roding Valleys and is famous for its hornbeams, lopped for centuries by the commoners of surrounding parishes; there are also grazing rights, now little used, for 2000 cattle. The Corporation of London, after an Act of 1878, became both landlord and conservator, in the latter role with the duty to continue the traditional woodland management, in the former to protect the rights of commoners while allowing free access to the public. Neither lopping nor pasturing occurs now in the woodland, scrub takes over grass (half the acreage since 1920) and the old, gnarled tree trunks send their broad shoots to heaven like gargoyles imitating angels.

In fact there are at least as many beeches as hornbeams, but they nearly always share the same ground and partake of the same character. Oaks, mostly pedunculate, were pollarded with the hornbeam and beech, and are scattered remarkably evenly throughout. Only holly and birch among the commoner trees show any remarkable distribution pattern; in fact the only pure stands in the forest are those of birch – some grown up from old coppice – and occasionally beech, which has some limited strongholds in the centre and the north-west. Hornbeam comes close to real dominance in the parts closest to Loughton and at Chingford; it tends to occupy the valleys of the turgid forest streams. There are several bogs and ponds, rich in rushes and horsetails.

The forest is unbelievably busy, even now that the M11 takes away most of the traffic. Nevertheless, it is a poetic and lovely woodland, and the poetry begins wherever you step away from a road. In its richness of form and depth of shade it seems to embody all that we expect of a forest. But each picturesque bole with its crown of tall, straight branches is a symbol: centuries of toil and use in the bole, one century of 'conservation' to create the top-heavy crown. There is too much shade. The ground is often bare; the hornbeams decay in the shade of their companion beeches, eventually becoming emaciated corpses amongst the cigarette cartons and beer cans. (Much larger rubbish is also dumped, and no less than 159 stolen cars were abandoned in the forest in 1982, most of them set on fire.) The Corporation of London made a noble gesture in the late nineteenth century when, finding itself the owner of rights of common (because

it owned a cemetery), it took the part of less-privileged commoners of Loughton who were fighting against the loss of their rights through inclosures. It has often been praised for the way it has administered this land outside its boundaries. But, for various reasons, no doubt outside its control, it has failed to perpetuate the wood-pasture character of the forest. Any day now I expect to hear that the forest has been handed over to the Forestry Commission with a brief to 'preserve its hardwood character while converting it to softwood production'. The Conservation Centre (behind the King's Oak at High Beach) is open every day except Mondays and Tuesdays.

You can walk anywhere at any time: use our map.

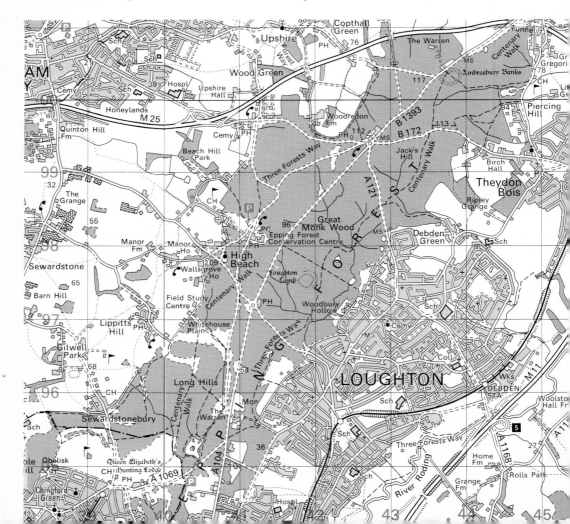

Old, typically burred oak with birch and hornbeam, Epping Forest

Pollard beeches and, BELOW, old coppice birch
in Epping Forest

Hainault Forest *475 925,* ♀ *, 1000 acres*
approximately, CP(GLC)
There are various waymarked woodland walks
on this reafforested common. The picnic area
is in open parkland by a lake, with various
facilities including a café, all indicated by an
insignificant symbol on the A1112, 3 miles
north-west of Romford. Entrances at the
north-west side, from Manor Road, lead
directly into the woodland, with more walks.

SOUTH-EAST LONDON

Joyden's Wood *504 720,* ♀ ♠ *, 450 acres,*
easy walks and schools' trail, FC
This nearest to London (13 miles) of the
Forestry Commission's properties is a very
attractive wood, almost impossible to get to by
road. The main roads are designed to get you
away, and the local streets are extremely con-
gested. However, the National Bus 421 from
Belvedere to Swanley, via Bexley Post Office,
passes an entrance to the wood in Summerhouse Drive on the Joyden's Wood Estate. Or

you can walk ½ mile south from Bexley Station, entering via High Street and Vicarage Road. If you must go by car, the best way is to turn off the Maidstone Road, A20(T), just before Swanley (avoiding the bypass) by Birchwood Road through orchards and gooseberry fields, then left and uphill into Summerhouse Drive. There is no official car park. From all these directions you will infer that I think the wood is worth finding. It has indeed the authentic atmosphere of old Kentish woodland, and I was touched by the persistence here amongst the housing estates and flyovers of a quality I find hard to describe. Old chestnut coppice, aspens, sallows and very pretty birch trees, with honeysuckle and foxgloves, greet you as you embark on the schools' trail from Summerhouse Avenue, over sandy and uneven ground and before you get to the *raison d'être* of the wood, *Pinus nigra*, larch beyond.

Even closer into the labyrinth of central London are **Bostall Woods**, *466 780*, and **Lesnes Abbey Woods**, *477 787*, dark and overgrown and slightly parkified, but none the less beautiful and vivid reminders of a much more rural east London, where oak and chestnut had real meaning in everyday life.

Between Woolwich and Greenwich, near the Thames Barrier, is the tiny **Maryon Park**, *420 786*, clean and tidy, with lovely specimen trees: silver lime, Judas tree, purple hazel, willow-leaved pear, all around a quiet green. You can park in the streets on the south side.

South of Woolwich at Eltham is a largish complex of woods, common and park with **Oxleas Wood**, north and west of Falconwood Station, *446 755*; dense oakwoods looking unbelievably natural on each side of the A2.

Further south the small **Chislehurst Common**, *440 704*, is well wooded, with enough oak and birch, among some aliens, to convince you that you are in the country only 50 yards from a busy shopping street. A mile south-east towards Orpington is a seriously preserved woodland, Petts Wood.

Petts Wood *447 684*, ♀ , *88 acres, many easy paths, NT*
The Petts were Elizabethan shipwrights, but

Judas tree in Maryon Park, London SE7

most of the wood is called Willet Wood, after the local builder who pioneered Summer Time in the early years of this century. There is a Daylight Inn and a Willet Way – where the inhabitants of gingerbread Tudor houses have made good use of that extra hour in cultivating splendid gardens, many with a very distinctive velvety Lawson cypress cultivar dominating

Chislehurst Common

the front garden and giving an unusual unity to the street.

The wood is pretty, with much birch, some mature oak, some chestnut recently coppiced after a fifty-year gap. A very countrified ploughed field of the sandy, pebbly soil intervenes at the north but there is continuous woodland to St Paul's Cray Common – Chislehurst is beyond. Park in Birchwood Road, which is off Chislehurst Road, Orpington, at the point where it becomes Hazelmere Road, for a pedestrian entrance under the railway. Petts Wood Station is less than $\frac{1}{2}$ mile south.

Ide Hill *489 517,* ♀ *, easy short walk, NT*
Toy's Hill *465 517,* ♀*, easy routes, NT*
Approach either by Brasted, east of Westerham on the A25, or by the B2042 from Four Elms. Ide Hill has only an L-shaped sliver of woodland, but very pretty: beech and oak, pines and whitebeams. The path on the steep scarp is easy and provided with handrails and steps, and there is a stone seat. The hilltop view is

Summertime in Petts Wood

marvellous, framed by clumps of broom on a green sward, with benches under pines and beeches – a very good place for a picnic. The National Trust also provides a shaded field near the car park. The Old Rectory, enclosed by the L shape, has massive chestnuts, pines, cherries, and very noble-looking *Sequoia-dendron*. The village offers a shop, a coffee house and a pub, and one of the most undistinguished little churches I have ever seen, all round a nice village green.

A mile over the fields westwards is Toy's Hill – it is much further by road. Here is a large National Trust car park (where they charge for parking in the summer), the focal point of a group of National Trust woods rather confusingly intermixed with private estates. Octavia's Wood and Brasted Chart are on the dip slope, old beech and durmast oak coppice with some pollards, and there are some whitebeams – the wood is nice and simple with a bare leaf-litter floor. The twisted and bent shapes of the trunks tell their story of many centuries' exploitation. The more used trees

are, the more they seem to assume human shapes. The Chart was a common, a wood-pasture, where the sounds of axe and saw echoed daily as, no doubt, the swineherds' whistle, at least in autumn. The wood was used for charcoal for ironworks, and the faggots to dry hops, and of course to keep people warm. Mossy pits and hollows are the remains of old quarries for chert or chart-stone – the local equivalent of flint, and the origin of the peculiar name.

Octavia Hill was a lady whose sister Frances owned the land, which was one of the earliest acquisitions of the National Trust. There is a well dedicated to Octavia (she was a co-founder of the Trust).

Down House: Sandwalk Wood *432 612, ♀, 20 minutes' easy stroll, Royal College of Surgeons*
The house is open every afternoon except Monday and Friday. You have to be interested to see Darwin's reconstructed study, otherwise the walk works out at two pence per minute.

Octavia's Wood, Toy's Hill

Charles Darwin, author of *The Origin of Species*, lived here for 41 years and planted the wood with birch, wild cherry and holly. He made a sandy – now grassy – 'thinking path' which offers a choice of shade or sun, according to route. The wood is rather small and linear for a memorial to our greatest naturalist-philosopher, but it is at least authentic.

A most attractive bit of country lies south of New Addington, with oak-lined lanes and a wood on every hill. South of Woldingham are National Trust woodlands at **South Hawke**, *373 540*, escarpment beech, very grand but full of the noise of the M25 below and infiltrated by rough-riding motorcyclists – not quite the National Trust atmosphere. The motor road through the woods continues south and west, bridging the motorway to pretty Godstone and **Tilburstow Hill**, where there is a pleasant car park at *350 500*, with some quieter woods to walk in: old chestnut coppice grown up with beech, oak and sycamore on cliffs of red gravel. The point of the place is its view. None of these woods is large; added together as a drive they are impressive and the roads are surprisingly quiet outside commuter times.

There is more National Trust woodland north-west of Redhill, as follows.

SOUTH-WEST LONDON

Gatton Park Wood *264 523*, ♀, *150 acres, many easy paths, NT*
Mostly on chalk are beech and ash with, in hollows, rhododendron and sycamore; horses churn the paths in the woods and motorbikes polish the ground of an old quarry. There are nice views, lots of red campion and wood sanicle: but it all needs taking in hand. There are some bluebells and even a bank with a few white helleborines. Turn south from the M25 onto the A217 then immediately left and right for the parking ground.

Margery Wood and **Colley Hill** *246 523*, ♀, *easy path to the North Downs, NT*
Unfortunately the M25 is to go smack through the middle of Margery Wood. I expect there

The rape of Margery Wood

will be a footbridge, but I would have insisted on a deep cutting with a roof carrying soil, and the trees replaced. Why should a road be more important than a wood?

The trees are oaks with birch and aspen, and the path emerges onto a grassy down with masses of hawthorn and a splendid view. From here and from other viewpoints on the North Downs you have the impression that Surrey is about 75 per cent trees: statistically it is 15 per cent woodland, twice the national average, but this takes no account of hedgerow and garden trees. Margery Wood is 20 miles from London off the A217, $\frac{1}{3}$ mile east of the junction with the M25. There is a decent place to park.

Kew Gardens *184 775*, ♀ ♠, *300 acres, 2m minimum walking, easy but can be exhausting, MAFF*
Properly the Royal Botanic Gardens, Kew, Surrey, and administered by the Ministry of Agriculture, Kew Gardens has been a national botanic garden since 1841, much enlarged by its great first director, Sir William Hooker. It is in a class of its own. For woodland, Kew might seem a tame resort; but it is amongst other things a comprehensive collection of temperate trees, and it breathes a woodland air. Autumn leaves and fruits, winter-flowering trees, in spring the early magnolias, and all the native trees in bud and shoot, fine pines, spruces and oriental conifers generally, even a bluebell wood in spring, and a great collection of flowering cherries; in summer a powerful orchestration of leaf and blossom: and all easily

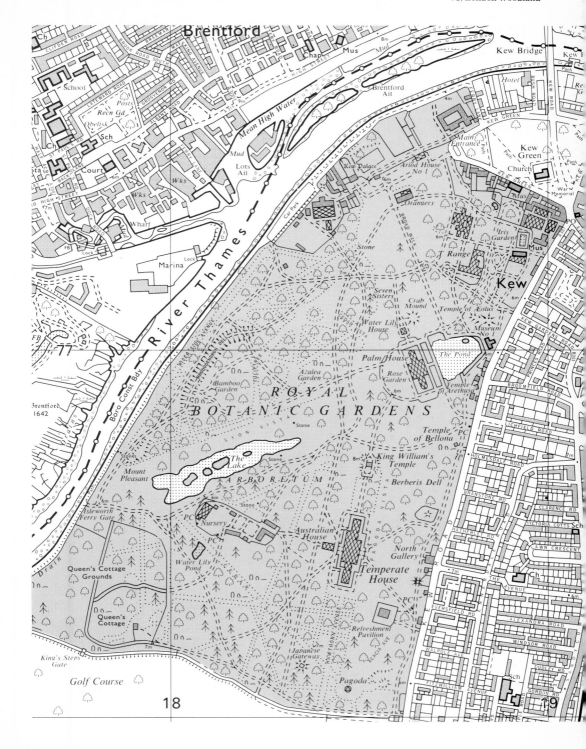

Brentford

Kew Bridge

Kew

Church

Kew Green

Main Entrance

Kew Palace

Orangery

Seven Sisters

Crab Mound

Temple of Æolus

Water Lily House

Museum No 1

Palm House

The Pond

ROYAL BOTANIC GARDENS

Rose Garden

Azalea Garden

Temple of Arethusa

Bamboo Garden

Temple of Bellona

King William's Temple

The Lake

Stone

Mount Pleasant

ARBORETUM

Berberis Dell

Isleworth Ferry Gate

Nursery

Australian House

North Gallery

Queen's Cottage Grounds

Water Lily Pond

Temperate House

Queen's Cottage

Refreshment Pavilion

King's Steps Gate

Japanese Gateway

Golf Course

Pagoda

River Thames

Mean High Water

Marina

Wharf

School

Court

Brentford 1642

Boro Const Bdy

18

19

accessible via Kew Gardens Station on the District Line. For drivers out of London the roads can be off-putting. Out of rush-hour times the Hammersmith–Great West Road route will serve. The parking place indicated by the map reference is reached by turning down Ferry Lane from the north side of Kew Green.

A TREE WALK
The gate from the car park takes you straight into mature arboretum country: *Zelkovas* and a few but interesting remains of the elm collection, including *Ulmus villosa*, the hairy-fruited Himalayan elm. Keeping close to the river you progress through oaks of many different origins – cork oak surrounded by English wild flowers – to the magnificent pine section. Don't miss the lacebark pines. A pair of towering Leyland cypresses signals the route into the rest of the conifer section; or keep right and towards the riverside for the Queen's Cottage Grounds and a close approach to native woodland, bluebells in season. Either

way you are sure to find many extraordinary and interesting conifers before emerging into deciduous woodland trees.

Returning, aim for the informal woodland area round the nursery, *Nothofagus* to the south, *Paulownia* tucked away in a corner, an ancient hornbeam and some unexpectedly fine-boned rhododendrons. The roadway, actually labelled Woodland Walk, then takes you north-eastwards by large sweet chestnuts to the head of the lake: crossing the grass you can plunge into a densely wooded patch, supposedly devoted to the ash family, but with the botanical serendipity you will have learned already to expect at Kew. At the edges see the oldish *Magnolia × soulangiana* and *campbellii*, then strike through the great beeches and American poplars north to the Brentford Ferry Gate by which you entered. On the map you will have covered little over a mile, but something about the low, flat land and, in my case, the very frequent pauses and detours, makes Kew Gardens very tiring. It really is a complicated place and it is best not to try and

The pines at Kew Gardens

see too much in one expedition. You might of course take food or eat at the Refreshment Pavilion, then take one of the routes outlined below.

AN APRIL WALK
Enter by the Victoria Gate – this is the one nearest to Kew Station.

A *Magnolia* section is immediately to your left. Crossing to King William's Temple you may not be too late for the flowers of *Parrotia persica*, a rich rusty brown on grey twigs, appropriate to a tree called Persian ironwood. *Hammamelis* species are here, blue tits posing amongst the crumpled strips of blossom, and the native Cornelian cherry may still be in bloom. Beyond the shrubbery is a large and impressive *Magnolia kobus* which carries so many flowers that it looks like a tree with shining white leaves.

Now turn to the north, or if there is no sun, roughly to the rear of the great Palm House. Here the Japanese cherries are arranged in a fairly compact group. All, except the wild hill cherry, *Prunus serrulata* in its natural form, found in 1822, were introduced from Japan in the early years of this century, so they have benefited from an organized planting programme. *P. sargentii* and *P. × yedoensis* are the most striking trees amongst many. Yeddo was the old name of Tokyo.

Keeping the Palm House on your right, circle round it to the Woodland Garden – a successful attempt to recreate a corner of British woodland – and the Rock Garden. This is of course not woodland, but a careful inspection will reveal at least two of the native herbaceous willows and some 'trees' of *Betula nana*, the dwarf birch, which you are not likely to see south of the Scottish Highlands – unless you know your way about Upper Teesdale, where you will find the only station where this alpine is native to England.

Returning to Victoria Gate by The Pond, note the well-formed and large Turkey oaks. You could have walked only a mile if your course was unwavering.

IN SUMMER
The Lion Gate at the south-east corner is

Wisteria, grown on a Victorian iron frame, Kew

convenient for the conifers, where I hesitate to guide you: if you are into exotic conifers you don't need me. I would only suggest that on one of those long, hot London summer days, the cypress grove just south-west of the intersection between the Oak Avenue and Cedar Vista is about the best place, not to walk, but to rest. On a less hot day you might cross the Syon Vista to seek the Azalea Garden and Tulip Tree Avenue; here on a slight rise are the sometimes magnificent Virginian ironwood or hop-hornbeam and other *Ostrya* species. You will see many fine things on the way – *Catalpas*, particularly, are a speciality at Kew.

AN AUTUMN WALK
Autumn can be a long season in a mild year at Kew, and December is not too late. The Lion Gate again gives easy access to an open woodland of hickory, horse-chestnut, *Robinia* and, above all, maple (east of the Temperate House). From the great golden Norway maple near the house to the intricately patterned snakebark maples here is a great richness of tree forms; and of course the only things you can gather at Kew are fallen leaves and fruits. Perhaps I am childish in valuing Japanese and other maple leaves, which have retained surprisingly rich colours after many years, between the pages of a blank book.

Turning back, wander in and out of the *Sorbus* and hawthorn sections which lie to the south of the Temperate House: many decorative fruits are to be seen, and beyond towards the darker pines and evergreen southern beeches of the so-called Mosque Hill you will find *Prunus subhirtella* 'Autumnalis' in flower.

IN WINTER

There is always something to see, but if it is cold resort to the Australian House. You would hardly expect woodland under glass, but in this small and beautifully laid out house is what seems to me, in ignorance, an authentic atmosphere created by the dry, scented eucalyptus and acacia and other Antipodean plants, many, of course, flowering in our winter.

It is impossible to predict which, but various spruce cones can be unexpected delights of a winter walk, and the tits and finches are even more willing than usual to share your snack.

Do not leave your visit to the gardens until late in the day; closing time is at sunset. However, the gardens are open every day of the year and only cost ten pence (and probably will do for some time) to enter. One disadvantage of Kew, which does not seem to affect the trees, is the almost continuous roar of jet planes to or from Heathrow. There are some theories that noise and even the tramping of feet stimulate the growth of trees; Kew seems not to disprove these.

> And you shall wander hand in hand
> With love in summer's wonderland:
> Come down to Kew in lilac-time
> (It isn't far from London!)
>
> Alfred Noyes

Syon House, across the river, also has a notable collection of specimen trees. Sadly there is no longer a ferry from the Isleworth Gate of Kew to the London Apprentice, and that gate is now closed.

Chiswick House, *210 775*, Palladian with a now-sprawling *Cedrus libani* avenue, has a bit of woodland (with guelder rose), and **Osterley Park**, *147 774*, house by the Adam brothers, is noted for large Hungarian oaks; there is also a rather tatty woodland fringe. Both parks are easily got to by the Great West Road, A4.

Richmond Park: Isobella Plantation
205 718, ♀ (♠), 50 acres, 1m, very easy, Royal Park

Two or three paths by streams planted with woodland trees provide a charming woodland walk in the middle of the Deer Park: old oaks also in the park to the south. Not all is the result of careful horticulture; there are some old trees and a hint or two that this was once a working coppice. Many picturesque old trees, when I visited, were merely shadows in a gloomy London fog. On a brighter day this woodland garden, so designated, can be strongly recommended. The parking place indicated is large and now planted with trees, the woodland being downhill to the west, across the road. Large trees near the car park are sweet chestnut with good nuts in late autumn. The Robin Hood Gate is the nearest.

December, Isobella Plantation

Wimbledon Common *230 725, ♀ , 1100 acres, up- and downhill paths in all directions, LA*

This extraordinary piece of rough, gravelly hillside, partly covered by birchwood, has had a strong appeal to many Londoners as an accessible wilderness. How did it come to be there? I have skated on Wimbledon's ponds and walked on its varied paths in all seasons without ever asking this question. The earliest name, Winebeald's Dun, tells us little; Dun is a down or lesser mountain, not apparently a dune, which might refer to the sandy nature of the heath. Most of it was the Common of the

Manor of Wimbledon when the Lord of the Manor, Lord Spencer, decided to split up the land and with the proceeds of the sale of one part, fence and preserve the other as a public park – with a residence for himself in the middle. The commoners were thought to be too few to protest, and the justification for Lord Spencer's action was the poor state of the common, full of rubbish, gypsies and tramps, often encroached upon and torn about by excessive gravel digging. But the commoners turned out to be numerous and vociferous and would have none of the Spencer proposal even though he virtually established his legal right to dispose of the land. Influenced by a House of Commons' enquiry into London's open spaces, both parties managed to agree in 1870. His Lordship gave up his rights in return for a perpetual £1200; and eight conservators, five elected by the ratepayers, were to control the common – which they still do.

As for a woodland walk, you will only rarely be out of sight of a bus route, so set a course down the middle and follow your nose into the woodland to the right or left. The grid reference is for the windmill, where there is a car park.

OTHER SURREY COMMONS

Surrey is well known for its commons and open spaces and those nearer to London are, like Wimbledon, characteristically sandy heaths with birches and some pines, open rather than wooded. But others are on patches of London clay and are oakwood, with hazel coppice or as wood-pasture, both nowadays overgrown. As with all surviving commons in built-up areas there is unrestricted access, so that many paths are made, some formally by the County Council, many more casually. But there is no grazing to keep the scrub down. The clay commons make for very difficult walking in winter, especially as horse riders do not always keep to the scheduled rides. Surrey wooded commons within 15 miles of Westminster are Esher, Ashstead and Epsom, with Great Bookham a little further out.

Ashstead Common *183 612,♀, 458 acres, 1 gravel path, many others, usually muddy, LA*
Oaks and bracken are the dominant vegetation, varied by birch, sallows and grey poplars. Bluebells are extinct through over-picking. The main pathway explores the margin between the oakwood of Ashstead and the wet pasture of Epsom Common to the north-east, where much birch thicket is developing. There are lovely patches of the common rush as well as the (actually more common) other *Juncus* species by two ponds near the parking place on the B280. Fishing is allowed in the pond nearer the road and there is a focus of popular interest here. Very few people, even on a fine June Sunday, penetrated even as far as the second pond. Patches of tormentil enliven the pathways.

Great efforts are made to keep pony riders to their proper tracks, but a few semi-wild ponies, New Forest style, would actually much improve the environment. Nonetheless there is a lovely interplay of green light in the woods and sky light in the birch heath, and it is a happy place. The parking ground is pleasant but too small.

Great Bookham Common *134 569,♀, 300 acres, many paths, NT*
The road on the east side, south from Stoke D'Abernon, is lined with rich houses no doubt occupying the sites of squatters' cottages dating from the seventeenth century, when the practice of the poor or displaced was to build

Ashstead Common and a June sky

their houses in one day and, having smoke
from their chimneys the next morning,
establish their right to be there – not in fact
legally. One parking place is closed because of
persistent rubbish dumping and the other, at
the map reference, is not easy to see. There is
also a parking place at the north-west. The
wood is a solemn timber oakwood with hazel,
mostly a wilderness with one or two patches
cleared where foxgloves grow. I found it just a
little oppressive, but you may find differently.

Box Hill *180 513, many walks, slippery in
winter, NT*

> Into a warm electric train
> Which travels sorry Surrey through;
> And crystal-hung the clumps of pine
> Stand deadly still beside the line.

From *Uncollected Poems* by John Betjeman

Sorry Surrey it may seem if we swing from the
A24 to the parking ground below Box Hill,
where there are actually fruit machines. Back
left from the roundabout with its gawdy hotel
you will find the National Trust zig-zag road,
barely signposted, which leads up to two large
parking places on the hilltop. Here you will not
be too surprised to find a licensed restaurant
attached to the Trust shop. There is a modest
charge for parking.

Follow the trail of sweet papers and empty
cans to a fine beechwood with many yews and
some straggly box trees. The effect of the pale
beech trunks against the black-green yews is
fine, and perhaps now unique in this part of the
country. Box trees are always pretty. You
almost never see a straight one, but even from
the timber point of view this is all right because
boxwood is used only in very short lengths.
Supplies for wood engravers are now imported
from the Mediterranean – quite unnecessarily
if it were not for the fact that we have
exterminated or neglected our boxwoods. It is
true that, since engravers use the end grain, a
large block has to come from a comparatively
broad trunk. But Victorian engravers produced
millions of large illustrations by piecing
together small squares of wood: surely the
pattern of joints, when it shows on an under-

inked print, is acceptable. I do not believe that
wood engraving will die out or be driven out by
computer draughtsmanship or anything else,
so why not, forestry experts, increase our own
supplies of box? But no doubt we shall
continue to take the line of least resistance, and
pay out to the Turks. Just one more bit of
special pleading: boxwood instruments and
tools are now collectors' items fetching large
sums. Of course, plastic is accurate, and
replaceable when it breaks . . .

Ranmore Common *143 502,* ♀♣, *715
acres, NT*
Abinger and Friday Street are signposted from
Dorking, but the nearer Ranmore Common

Box Hill beeches

and Denbies Hillside are not. The common stretches back a mile or more from the ridge north of the A25, and can be reached by aiming for Dorking Town Station to the north-west of the town. The common is what is called good walking country and is picturesque; Polesden Lacey adjoins to the north and can be reached from Westhumble.

Norbury Park *166 522*, ♀ ♠, *300 acres, open, LA*

For Norbury Park and the heavily wooded ridge facing Box Hill across the ever-noisy A24, go by Crabtree Lane just beyond Westhumble Station. There are no encouraging signposts, but there is in fact a

BOX

Its Roman name *Buxus* included flutes, tops and combs – it is the seeds that are in precious brown boxes. The musical snap of my parallel rules is as clean as the millions of lines, printed without wearing out, of Victorian cuts. These often imitated the flourishing pen lines of Academicians, carefully cut around by myopic men – who sometimes got into the Academy too. In gardens, box topiary also creates images, but I wish there were still woods for all the suburban Boxwood Avenues.

picnic site near the Druids Grove, *156 533* – a once-famous collection of old yews now in some disarray. With the busy road below, thoughts of druids, always anyway an eighteenth-century fiction, are far away. There is a good metalled roadway through Norbury Park, and this can be a relief when the rides are muddy. The park is administered by Surrey County Council and quite open to walkers: beechwoods are a little sad but there are a couple of healthy wych elms.

This, with the woods described in Section 14, completes the circular perambulation of Dorking, but only hints at the many surprises awaiting walkers. Certainly, I completely changed my attitude to 'sorry Surrey'.

South of East Horsley is the **Effingham Forest**, which the Forestry Commission calls East Horsley Woodlands. On each side of Honeysuckle Bottom are the dark woods of Dick Focks Common and Mountain Wood, the roads crossed in places by bridges carrying trees (so the one-time landowner could walk in uninterrupted woodland). The main parking place is in Green Dene, *091 510*, which forks south-west from Honeysuckle Bottom. It all sounds very quaint, but in fact it is dull and dark, and, in spite of everything the Forestry Commission says in leaflets, dedicated 99 per cent to timber production. Honeysuckle Bottom is heavily settled, with all the houses painted whiter than white.

The **Sheepleas**, the County Council Open Space which shares the Green Dene car park, is largely an old sheep walk but has woodland with mature beech in places. There are two other car parks: on the Epsom road, A246, at West Horsley, *088 527*, and down a side road to the west, *085 514*.

There are many other open spaces and commons. I will only mention **Wisley Common**, *077 588*, and **Ockham Common**, *078 586*, divided by the A3(T) and with several car parks as well as the Royal Horticultural Society's Gardens, Wisley, *065 584*. Here again are the infertile Bagshot Sands – and yet the gardening centre of England flourishes, admittedly strong on *Erica* and *Calluna*, but with room for an arboretum in its 300 acres.

North Kent and South Essex

Landranger sheets 175, 177, 187, 188

Oak and beeches in picturesque decay, Knole Park

SEVENOAKS

Knole Park *540 543*, ♀ (♠), *1000 acres, LA (House NT)*

There used to be a Wildernesse at Knole, but it is now a golf links with tame deer and a few ancient oaks. The name has been given to a nearby housing estate – a touch of planners' irony perhaps. The park adjoins the town, and five minutes' walk takes you in. Parking in the town or at the house is expensive, and it is worth remembering that you can enter the park from several points around its 6-mile perimeter.

Woodland tends to be at the edges, but parkland on this massive scale is in a category of its own. It seems permanent, a vast broad composition, using trees and grassland like giant building blocks or simplified cardboard cut-outs. But of course it has been growing

into this shape for three centuries; on closer investigation the very mature character of the 'clumps' is revealed, each great beech or chestnut practically a wood in itself with dead limbs and even dead brothers lying about in picturesque decay. In fact, the trees which look so inevitably and permanently massed together from a distance are nearing their ends, and since the park is stocked with fallow deer there is little hope of natural regeneration. There are some fenced-in stands of conifers.

In the smoothed-out Wildernesse the ancient stag-headed oaks are also doomed to die alone unless the owners (the house only is National Trust) embark on some form of management apart from just mowing the grass and collecting venison.

You can walk where you like, when you like. There is no need for rubber boots unless you are very adventurous and the season is

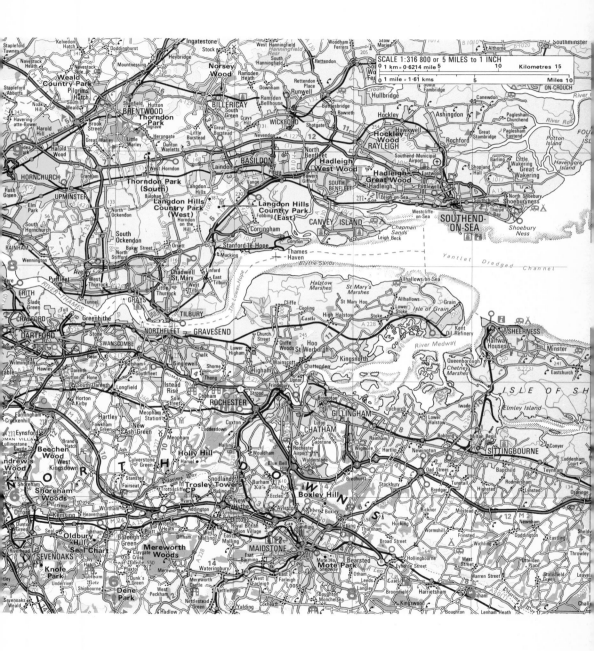

unusually wet. Deer tracks through the bracken usually bring you to easier paths in whatever direction you choose. The map reference is for the parking place near the house; it is not a bad place to start a walk, but you have to pay.

Andrew's Wood *502 615*, ♀ ♣, *1½m, easy, muddy, FC*

Shoreham and Badgers Mount are villages north of Sevenoaks, and Shoreham is of course the better known. Andrew's Wood is ¼ mile east of the roundabout junction of the A21 and A224, so it can be reached by looking out for this junction from London or Sevenoaks. It can also be reached from Shoreham. It is a

A birch at the side of Andrew's Wood supports the wild *Clematis*, traveller's joy

Norway maple leaves, Andrew's Wood

decent-sized mixed plantation on the hilltop, where pockets of clay in the chalk provide soils suitable for oaks, Norway spruce and Norway maple. Old yews and beeches and well-used chestnut stools indicate the former character of the wood, and there is a stand of close-set young beech; all the trees are ready for thinning. Maple provided the main subject for my camera, since I had not before seen it as woodland. It is very variable in leaf shape – a maple characteristic. The leaf is recognizable enough by its peculiar concave spines, in whatever number: usually three for each of five lobes. The bark is smooth, evenly ridged, like a greenish-grey fabric. As its name suggests it is not a native tree, but like some other Forestry Commission favourites it was plentiful in Britain before the Ice Age – it simply failed to make it back before the Dogger Bank and the English Channel were submerged. In a way it is more a native than any of us: it is not endemic to Norway.

All paths lead back to the parking place, except for one cross-ride, and a level terrace along the edge of a hillside, here facing east across a smooth chalk valley. Beyond the next hill lies little Shoreham, where Samuel Palmer's church is, but not much of his celebrated atmosphere. Here at the terrace edge are dogwood, buckthorn, whitebeam, yew, and birches hung with traveller's joy. A footpath crosses the valley to another stand of Forestry Commission trees, Shoreham Woods, then downhill again to the village.

The car park at Andrew's Wood is much used by dog walkers in the daytime and take-away eaters in the evening – the dogs being apparently much tidier. The wood is nicely managed and productive, serene and wrapped in its own sweet breath – not sour and neglected. The self-important howl of traffic beyond is almost muted.

North of Badgers Mount the woods continue to Hollows Wood; acres of chestnut coppice with muddy rides, occasional large beeches, oaks and birches, some hazel, some holly. Seemingly in disarray, with broken gates and decaying 'Private' notices, they are in fact cut for the chestnut paling industry. The lanes, particularly Shoreham Lane from Chelsfield,

490 630, are steep and pretty with arching foliage and gnarled roots of wayside beeches, hedged or coppiced in the past, on mossy banks. But the noise of the A21(T) penetrates everywhere.

Shoreham Woods, on the ridge nearer to Shoreham and ½ mile across the fields from Andrew's Wood, are quiet, and are controlled by the Forestry Commission. This is a nearly mature beechwood invaded by sycamore.

Approaching Shoreham Woods from the village itself – that is, turning left if you approach from the A225 – you can park, near a bus stop, before Filston Farm with its impressive oast house dwellings, *515 609*. The path is very steep, but there is more than a hint of Palmer's bountiful countryside in the *Clematis*-hung hedgerow trees and the billowing shapes of the beeches against a green meadow. Someone has hopefully planted elm – replanted I suppose – along the orchard side. Half way up the side of the wood is a stile, and

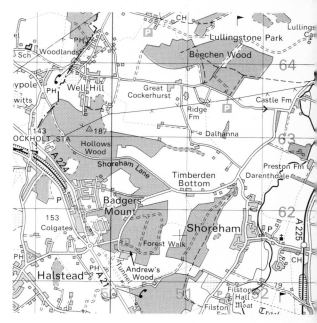

A hornbeam grove in Beechen Wood, near Shoreham

the footpath continues at right angles into the wood: level enough along the hillside. You can descend to one of Shoreham's three pubs before plodding back along the road.

Beechen Wood *516 637, ♀, easy, LA*

Lullingstone Park, north of Shoreham, is managed by Sevenoaks Borough Council, and cleverly combines a large golf course with a very interesting fragment of woodland. An open car park, *516 637*, leads one into a belt of overgrown chestnut coppice which, not very attractive in itself, serves to shelter a wilderness of the first order, municipal though it may be. Towering beeches and hornbeams are dwarfed only by the massive trunks of earlier specimens lying on the ground, and they are surrounded by thickets of their own offspring. Gaps are full of dead hulks overrun by brambles and willow herb, but with new trees growing spontaneously everywhere. Lovely! – and very good bird land, even though patrolled by a great variety of dogs every day.

Trosley Towers Country Park *644 613, ♀ (♠), 160 acres, many walks, some steep, LA*

North-east of Sevenoaks, where the M20, A20(T) and M26 meet deafeningly under the escarpment cliff with the much quieter Pilgrims' Way or North Downs Way, you can turn off northwards on the A227 to Vigo Village where Trosley Towers Country Park, 160 acres, lies behind the village, clearly signposted. Trosley is really the local way of pronouncing Trottiscliffe. There is a woodland parking area and a choice of three waymarked walks which wind along this heavily wooded, steep escarpment. The Pilgrims' Way is here a name for the lane below; the North Downs Way Long Distance Path passes above. As with all ancient routes there are several roughly parallel paths where beasts and men have avoided hazards such as mud and fallen trees.

This is a great place for natural shape and form, and a play of dark and light against an inspiring view of the Medway Valley. There is a whole gamut of woodland, from mature park plantation among old native trees through

Trottiscliffe church from Trosley Towers

overgrown coppice and new-cut coppice, ragged thicket and shattered yew, to a rich chalk scrub with wayfaring trees, whitebeam, maple and privet. As you emerge from the dark, cool woods to the steep, grassy down the wide view southwards is dominated by the small geometric shape of a church in the fields. The marked walks are a bit overdone perhaps, especially as there are footpaths wandering everywhere, although at least one of the walks is quite tough and 7 miles long. One or two of the trees near the car park have name-plates hanging on them as on sherry decanters. Hornbeam appears to be a well-established native on this chalk hill, which must hold pockets of clay. There are old yews and very

very long history of woodland management.

You can follow a level, terraced path along the hillside, or descend by rough steps to the lower slope – any height you lose is regained at the expense of your calf muscles. The park is closed at sundown, but since the village roads run along the back of the woods you can find an entrance – there is nothing to stop you walking in. I met a horse bearing a lantern at each stirrup – a strange pilgrim in the dusk; but, surely, not a new sight on this ancient ridge path.

Holly Hill, *670 629,* has a neat square of gravel to park in, guarded by a little cottage, and some humble sycamores and horse-chestnuts. The car park was made by a local gentleman, perhaps to discourage further exploration of the quiet lane. There *is* woodland, little more than a shelter-belt between fields. A great beech and some grown-up chestnut coppice show that it is a fragment of the large woodland of this downland. The walk here is breezy and light, and several children who arrived when I did seemed to find it promised sufficient adventure. Eastwards, down the steep Birling Hill, by Crookhorn Wood, the lane tunnels through native trees to industrial Snodland on the Medway.

Oldbury Wood *576 558,* ♀ *(♠), 2m walks, NT*
North of Ightham Common on the A25, 4 miles east of Sevenoaks, there is a neat and capacious car park set among slender birch trees, deep in a hollow. It serves Oldbury Hill, a prehistoric earthwork cared for by the

old beeches and fairly ancient coppiced stools of hazel and chestnut. It is chestnut which is being cut now, probably for palings, and in such clearings are revealed the grotesque twisted knots of traveller's joy, untidy drifts of willow herb and, at this late season, sinister globules of deadly nightshade and full-blown heads of great burdock. Birch and hawthorn are not always included in the coppices and there are some venerable individuals; also some oaks left as standards, more for their picturesque qualities than any remote likelihood of use for timber. At the far end of the wood I found very old stools of hornbeam, ash, birch and sallow – the last producing enormous leaves. Obviously this wood has a

National Trust. This is perhaps the most beautiful of Sevenoaks' woodlands: old oak coppice with beech and birch, bilberry, bracken, buckthorn, alder, sallow and rowan; hardly any chestnut. The birches are grey with lichen and there are subtle tones of grey in all the colours; all are seen against the dark side of the valley. There are many fungi and a nice smell of decaying damp leaves.

Seal Chart, *566 557*, westwards, also has pleasant oak woodland with bracken; here the oaks are middle-aged standards. The common is open to all.

Ightham Common, south across the A25, is

Alder buckthorn among birches in the wood below Oldbury Hill

all nice houses; the lanes are lined with native hedgerow trees and many gardens have fine specimen trees. A tulip tree seemed to radiate light on a damp October morning, and in November still had some of its translucent yellow leaves. There are tall black pines and well-grown Lawson cypresses, as well as the

native oak. Amongst the capacious gardens I glimpsed a well-protected nut orchard. A woodland walk in suburbia might be the answer when it is too wet for the woods themselves. Ightham Mote, a mile further south, is a very old house, a veritable eye-full of quaint shapes and structures, open in summer. Notices threaten damage to your car if you block a gateway.

Dene Park *605 511*, ⚹ *(♀)*, *forest walk, FC*
This is part of the Forestry Commission's Shipbourne Forest, a dreary circuit of twenty-year-old spruces on paths of yellow Wealden slime, served by a very dirty car park. There are patches of oak and chestnut coppice and some beech. The most interesting bit is across the road where a fine old oakwood is planted with young Norway spruce, Norway maple, red oak and Japanese larch – a typical Forestry Commission cocktail, riotously coloured in autumn against the tweedy browns of the oaks. All the underwood is to be thinned to leave a stand of pure oak, and I hope we shall be allowed to walk there. Until then, northbound travellers from Tonbridge are advised to look towards Sevenoaks.

MAIDSTONE

Boxley Hill *775 590*, ♀, ⚹ *(yew)*, *3m of escarpment woods, part LA*
Box and yew are native on the very steep chalk scarp 2 miles north-east of Maidstone. The

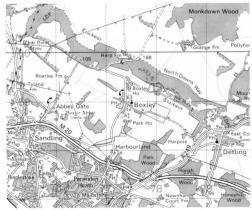

box seems to be a little thin on the ground but the yews are fine. As I arrive, a round, white moon rises amongst a flock of small clouds. Below the ridge the crowded trees are cocooned in old man's beard, which glistens in the moonlight. In the opposite direction, Maidstone and the motorway are marked by skeins of yellow light. There is the noise of twentieth-century man, rushing to the pub, or home to read to the children, or to his death. Which is real? Nature, especially by the light of a full moon, seems the stronger. We need the woods to stop us going mad – but we need the roads to get us to the woods.

This is not, however, a place to explore by moonlight, for the yews are dark even in daytime. The Pilgrims' Way here is a narrow metalled road along the foot of the Downs, and at the west end of this road there is a rough parking space for modern pilgrims. The path is very worn where it leads upwards, tunnelling beneath the ancient yews. The climb is worth the effort. In the spaces between the yews are old coppiced hazels, hawthorns and whitebeams, richly diversified in form. Spindle trees, leaning away from the shade of the ever-vigorous yews, are overturned but continue to fruit in abundance. Native privet fills every gap. Dog's mercury covers the ground.

Towards the top, yew gives way to pedunculate oak, and there are many wild maples, unusually large, which in autumn cover the ridge paths with gold. Here the going is easy, in and out of the heavy, sheltering

Fungus and dog's mercury under a coppiced hazel in the Boxley yew wood

Field maple by the Pilgrims' Way

yews. In the perpetual dryness beneath them, large round mushrooms or blewits, brown with age, are marked with sinister double crosses. This fungus is at first a delicate brown-pink, deckled at the edges like an antique Doulton dish; many together are spread out like a dinner service.

Along the Pilgrims' Way eastwards beyond Boxley House are open beechwoods invaded by various maples and birch. An ancient hollow way leads uphill, past a quarry, then shaded by beech, yew and whitebeam, to the narrow North Downs Way which runs muddily between poor scrub (with elder and birch) and extremely healthy root crops in the level fields beyond the slope. A more sudden change of countryside character can hardly be imagined than from the scarp to this flat land.

There seems to be nowhere to park along the top of the ridge. Large woods to the north-east are isolated in farmland, but the lanes by Bredhurst are charmingly narrow and overgrown.

Mote Park, in the eye of Maidstone itself, is large and old, and remarkable for some very large and unusual trees, among them the largest field maple probably in the world, 78 feet, and black walnut, 97 feet by 19 feet. You may do better than I did and visit these great trees in daylight. The park closes at 7.30 pm and parking is reasonably priced. It is not woodland of course, though there are a lot of trees close together near the house to the east.

Mereworth Woods on the B2016 south of Wrotham Heath loom large on the map. Part is Forestry Commission and there are bridle-ways. The National Trust has a corner at the south, Gover Hill. The woods consist of miles and miles of chestnut coppice on the Weald, and conifers, but all with the old hedge banks. This is working woodland, good perhaps for horse riders. The countryside around is much more relaxed than in the downland, people not afraid of square corners on their roofs and walls, and not so worried about trespassers – though nut orchards of course have plenty of barbed wire. There are plenty of trees even without the elms, and a generally woodsy air in villages and lanes; a faintly detectable blue of wood smoke.

I had no idea there was so much chestnut in Kent. These 4 square miles of woodland must be the last hollow kernel of Andreasweald, which stretched from beyond Canterbury to Winchester and was 30 miles deep; a forest so dense, that the Romans, who named it SYLVA ANDERIDA, made only two small roads across it, preferring to sail round to LONDINIUM. If it was the Romans who introduced the chestnut, as some people believe, the seed has certainly found fertile ground in the nineteen centuries since they left.

NORTH OF THE THAMES

Brentwood, 22 miles from St Paul's, is an old town, once a small clearing in the Essex Forest where pilgrims on their way to Canterbury from East Anglia and the Midlands used to stop. Essex County Council has rescued considerable areas of parkland including old woodland to form the green belt – or green skirt – of what is now a large dormitory town.

Weald Country Park 574 946, ♀ ✦ , 428 acres, LA
The park was bought for £27,500 in 1953. Nineteenth-century conifer plantations felled during the war were then already replanted. The deer park to the south-east existed for 700 years before most of it was ploughed in 1948 to try to cash in on a war-time ploughing subsidy, rumoured, wrongly, to be due for removal. But many beautiful ancient oak, hornbeam and beech trees remain – some at least must be almost as old as the park itself. The deer were let loose by the Army during the war; fallow deer descendants are now wild visitors to the park. A belvedere, with a view of the dullest part of the park, is close to the site of the former house, which was demolished in 1950. On the slopes are well-grown specimen conifers and a group of particularly fine tall hornbeams.

The woodland part of the park is to the north, beyond an area known as the Forest, which used to be fenced as a sort of domestic wilderness. The woodlands were originally agricultural fields, the tenants expelled or bought out in the eighteenth century so that the land could be enclosed into the park.

Planting is well documented and much can be learned about how forestry trees grow. Older trees, described as 'canopy', tend to be picturesque but useless for timber and therefore left alone by past woodcutters. Native vegetation creeps in at the edges. Alder is luxurious by stream sides. The thinnings from the woodland are sold, but the object now is conservation, for public pleasure and instruction. Partly by design, and partly by the accident of the pleasantly varied shape of the land, the woodland rides make some of the prettiest walks to be found in south-east England.

There are four car parks: use the south one nearest to Brentwood for the deer park and the east one for the woodlands. A nice booklet is available from the town newsagent – or ask a warden for a leaflet map.

The woodlands occupy an area large enough to be effective as a habitat for badgers and for little owls, lesser spotted woodpeckers and tree sparrows. Canada geese are resident and naturalized on the lakes, and goosander and water rail have been recorded. But the lakesides are eroded by too many fishermen. The old deer park, steeply undulating with scattered ancient oaks, is very picturesque, and the whole atmosphere is cheerful and relaxed.

Thorndon Park lies to the south of Brentwood. It is really two parks. The larger northern section, with an extensive picnic area, *608 916*, amongst very pretty birches and picturesque old oaks, is reached by the B186, turning off at Eagle Way, or by the A128, turning down The Avenue. Close to a built-up area, this park at weekends is full of dogs, children, horses and lovers, but the old oaks are worth anyone's time. Woodland beyond the birch thicket is varied from oak with hornbeam or chestnut to beech according to minute changes in the texture, and no doubt acidity, of the yellow mud and gravel which the trees seem to love.

The venerable oaks of these Essex parks are remnants of one of the most extensive and long-established forests of England. Thorndon Park North is not, however, a mediaeval deer park but an old common, Childerditch; grazed, and its trees pollarded, since perhaps men first settled in the forest. Rackham (1980) quotes a survey of 1774 recording 2080 oak pollards and 1323 hornbeams: the latter are not so much in evidence now. The common was enclosed in 1774, and in latter years was neglected. (The house was gutted by fire in 1878.) Silver birch trees spread over the land. This explains the present mixture of venerable oaks and birch

Oaks in the Deer Park, Brentwood

Ancient woodland, Thorndon Park

thicket which characterizes the picnic area. Under some of the younger, not so densely shading oaks the ground is carpeted by seedlings – not that they have a chance to grow in the shade of the parent, but such excessive vigour is illustrative of oaks on Essex soil. Hawthorns, both the woodland and hedgerow species, are found here. The woodland or Midland hawthorn is the one with two seeds in the haw or berry – *Crataegus laevigata* or *oxyacanthoides*. There is a record from Thorndon of 21,000 hawthorns being grubbed up for the gardener's hedges.

Thorndon Park South, *632 899*, is older parkland with old pollard hornbeams. The hall itself may be reached by a footpath from Thorndon Park North. It is an impressive great barracks of a place which is now being converted into something useful.

Three miles east of Brentwood is Billericay, a well-known dormitory town. Billericay's Sunnymede is a collection of bright new houses whose occupants, exhausted by the exercise of their democratic and other responsibilities, may retire to Eggbreak Hill on the east side of the town, where Norsey Wood is run as a nature trail by the Borough Council.

Norsey Wood *692 957*, ♀, *165 acres, easy, wet, 1 hour, LA*
Although at first apparently solid sweet chestnut in various stages of growth after coppicing, this little wood also includes some old gravel pits with oak, hornbeam, and birch, and a system of wet valleys where the dominant tree is alder, with willows, and even some *Sphagnum* moss. Much of the oak is *Quercus petraea*. In the 1930s houses were built within the old area of the wood in the north-west and the south-west, obscuring a 'deerbank' (the wood was once, long ago, a deer park) which surrounded the whole, unchanged for four centuries. Rackham notes also a wide (70 feet) bank of unknown origin across the whole width of the east end. Roman kilns have been found, and there are Bronze Age barrows; the former suggest coppice to fire the kilns, the latter, eight or so centuries earlier, are likely to have been on open ground.

Perhaps too much emphasis is placed upon the evidence of occupation before the Middle Ages; but the wood just might have been chestnut coppice ever since the Roman (?) introduction of the tree. References to Norsey Wood, then Nossesheye or Notesheye, go back to 1250. The 'notes' might have been hazel-nuts – it is a more familiar mediaeval tree, but now rare in the vicinity. The largest chestnut stools cannot be dated earlier than the eight-eenth century, but pollen analysis, when it can be done, may provide the link.

Coppicing continues, at least in part of the wood, and the products are used on site in traditional ways. The nature trail is clearly marked by white engraved arrows on varnished posts, and takes one on a comprehensive tour of the whole range of woodland.

Near Basildon are **Langdon Hills Country Park West** and **East**, *680 865* and *697 860* respectively. These are instant parkland created out of surviving woodland and scrub. Two car parks, each with woodland, are acces-sible and signposted from the surrounding trunk roads and are linked by a very narrow lane and an extensive nature trail. This trail has two car parks of its own, and covers a great deal of open country and orchards as well as woodland. A notice-board map had been van-dalized and there was a lot of litter. The east car park is patronized for its tremendous view over the Thames to Kent, even, it seems, when the view is obscured by the weather. When visited in October the west park was closed; it is a large field.

SOUTHEND

Hadleigh West Wood *804 879,* ♀ *, several paths, LA*

An obscure notice-board and a rusty gate opposite Windsor Gardens mark the entrance to this wood. It is reputed to be very old and perhaps not even tamed or managed by the time of Domesday. But there are few signs of its age – some struggling wild service and the usual hornbeam stools and coppiced durmast oak – nor is there much sign that the wood is integrated into its urban surroundings. In fact the local people seem to avoid it. Very little coppicing is done. Bits of the edges are fenced into an adjacent field for cattle and horses to shelter. There is a great deal of chestnut and some aspen and, unusually, alder buckthorn, one tree 30 feet high. Several banks, apparently very old, lie across the width of the wood suggesting a once wider shape divided into east-west bands or strips. A deep stream flows west to east across the lower half and the only bridge is near the centre.

The value of this admittedly rare survival is surely in its accessibility to the dwellers in the housing estate which closes in on two sides. But people dump things, and no attempt has been made to provide parking or information. Anyone with a wood-burning stove in Hadleigh or Thundersley could have free fuel for a lifetime by simply picking up dead wood. Regular coppicing would supply somebody with an income from selling logs. Could not the borough council offer a licence plus a loan to buy a truck and a saw? Woods ought to be productive and underwood ought to be cut. It would make the place much more cheerful and vastly improve its ecology. The gloom on a fine sunny morning was only relieved at a natural clearing caused by a fallen chestnut. Much of the ground was covered by ripe chestnuts which were certainly good to eat because I roasted some, but no one had gathered any, or even walked that way for many days.

Hadleigh Great Wood, $\frac{1}{2}$ mile to the east, was probably once joined to West Wood. It is now deeply penetrated by detached residences, yellow sodium lights and rusting metal. There is hornbeam with oak standards, and again durmast oak, *Quercus petraea*. This wood is very much used compared to West Wood, for riding and dog walking at least. It is dank and overgrown.

Hadleigh Great Wood: leaves of sessile oak

Hockley Wood *834 924,* ♀ *, 350 acres, public park*

The old village of Hockley is now as large as a town, but much quieter than the main-road-ringed Hadleigh and Thundersley. The wood is a hornbeam coppice for most of its area, with tall oak and birch at the north, and some chestnut. I found a standard wild service among the hornbeam stools and several groups of aspen. Little coppicing is done and the wood is dark with the floor mostly quite bare. There are several ways into the wood from practically every one of the residential roads which border to the north and east. Walking is easy but occasionally very muddy. A certain monotony sets in even though the ground is uneven. A stream with mud banks runs down the east side. But in spite of the darkness and barrenness and a certain sameness it is a cheerful place which makes one glad it has been preserved as a town park. The council could improve the place by cutting the underwood – the sale of the logs should cover the cost. After all, hornbeam is the best wood fuel in the kingdom, after holly.

North Bucks with parts of Oxon, Herts and Beds Landranger sheets 152, 164, 165, 166

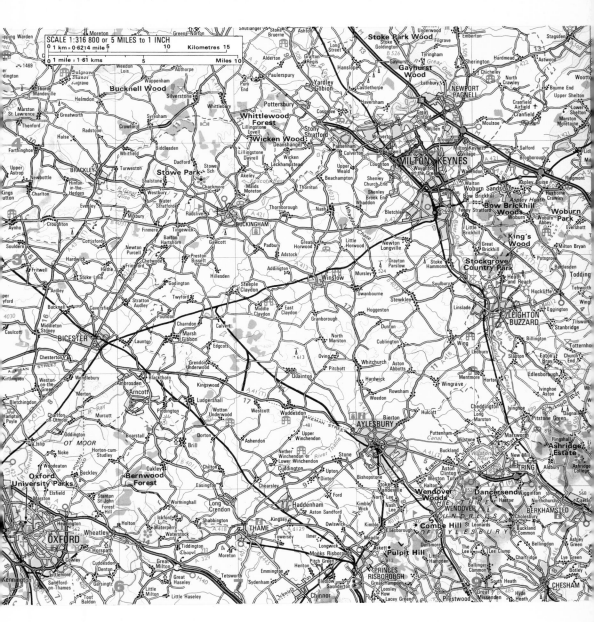

SCALE 1:316 800 or 5 MILES to 1 INCH

0   1 km = 0·6214 mile   5   10   Kilometres 15

0   1 mile = 1·61 kms   5   Miles 10

Near Oxford, and still on the Oxford Clay, is **Bernwood Forest**, *612 117*, the Forestry Commission's name for a plantation of softwoods which includes several old woods from **Waterperry** in the south to **Oakley** in the north. A sequestered car park is being prepared off the Oakley to Studley road – reached from Oxford by the Headington roundabout and Stanton St John. This is the only place you can leave a car.

These were ancient oakwoods, or ancient woods planted with oak, clear-felled in the last war. Native trees remain or are encouraged along rides, and the forest is described as a nature reserve because of its insect life. Birch, oak and wild service now flourish with a background of alien spruce. The rides are airy and well surfaced for walking – they also provide access for persons with nets and macro-lensed cameras to plunge into ditches. Will there still be space and suitable wet scrub for this activity when the forest grows to maturity?

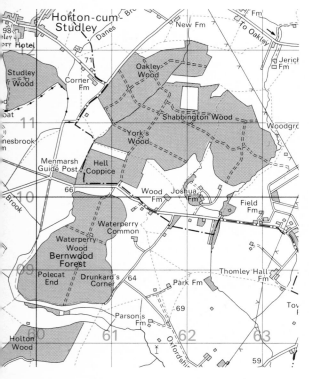

The **University Parks** in Oxford, while hardly woodland, have pleasantly informal corners as well as containing many fine specimen trees, native and exotic – well-documented in a reasonably priced guide available from Broad Street bookshops.

THE CHILTERN ESCARPMENT

Beechwoods on the Chilterns in Oxfordshire, Bucks and Herts are rarely ever fenced and offer easy walking, since mature beech always completely shades out the shrub layer. Chiltern scrubland in this section is especially rich in variety and of great ecological interest.

Ashridge Estate *973 130*, ♀ (♠ *phased out*), *4000 acres, many paths and waymarked trail, NT*
There are two large car parks, and others, and the B4506 runs through. Tring Railway Station is $1\frac{1}{2}$ miles to the west.

Tring, the home of the Royal Forestry Society (102 High Street), is the nearest town effectively, and the pretty village of Aldbury, with duck pond, at least one attractive pub and a good shop, lies in a hollow beneath the steep escarpment which is the great feature of the Ashridge Estate. On the hilltop, patches of sandy soil and clay-with-flint overlay the chalk, giving scope for a varied tree husbandry – and centuries of woodland management have left their peculiar patterns.

Ashridge may well have been an ash ridge long ago – ash trees to be found in the woods and as pioneers in the scrub – but the estate was famous for its beeches and oaks in the eighteenth century. Some old oaks remain on Aldbury Common, along with the lines of overgrown hawthorn hedges which are now used as private corridors by the herd of fallow deer. Muntjak and Chinese water deer are also established here. Great beeches are everywhere along the escarpment, as high woodland over typically bare leaf litter and in grotesque lopped forms on the old boundaries and lanes which criss-cross the estate.

At the least, this is a great beechwood with a view, traversed by an easy, dry bridleway which emerges onto the bare down towards

Ivinghoe Beacon at the north. But it is also a richly varied and large piece of woodland countryside which requires many days to reveal all its secrets: an old avenue of yews deep in the woods; a mature stand of sweet chestnut; a dense plantation of sycamore; heathland with bracken, birches, hollies and oaks; a group of tall aspens; a large bluebell wood, little frequented except by deer and birds; clay-filled hollows retaining water for much of the year and rich in mosses and rushes; many orchids and fungi for those who can seek them out. Over fifty species of bird actually breed in these woods.

Scrubland to the north is of pure hawthorn, but there is an interesting protected slope to the west on an outlying hill, *948 133*, where the grassy scrub is patterned with whitebeam, roses, and a mature buckthorn hedge. Here the succession from grass to woodland can be seen in progress, with ash as the pioneer tree in the full light at the edge of the beechwood. Again there is a surprise: a group of horse-chestnuts

far from their usual suburban surroundings.

To the south is a considerable area of heathland on Berkhamsted Common, down to the Gade Valley, where in Domesday times were at least two vineyards.

Ashridge is well known and attracts its thousands on a fine summer weekend, but the woods are scarcely disturbed. Looking out from the high beechwood you are at the still centre of a web of lines of communication. You may glimpse the prehistoric Icknield Way, deeply hollowed where it follows a contour of the hillsides. Below, in a deep cutting which is itself a monument of nineteenth-century engineering, runs the main-line railway from Euston to the North; beside it the Grand Union Canal, fed by the great reservoirs which usually gleam in the distance near Tring. The monument in the middle of Ashridge Estate is to the Duke of Bridgwater who built the first canal. You will see the chimneys of a modern industrial complex rooted in this chalky soil at Pitstone; the quarries are carefully restored to

Chilterns, January; red leaves on the beechwood floor; green algae on the trunks

grass. The ancient wooden windmill (National Trust) and the charming, lonely Pitstone church are not disturbed, except by a light deposit of white dust.

Ashridge is not remote or forbidding. There is even an open-air swimming pool at Ringshall, and along the B4506 you may see some startling examples of twentieth-century domestic architecture, as well as some very simple brick cottages. Another somewhat jarring element is the noisy kennels concealed somewhere below the monument. On bank

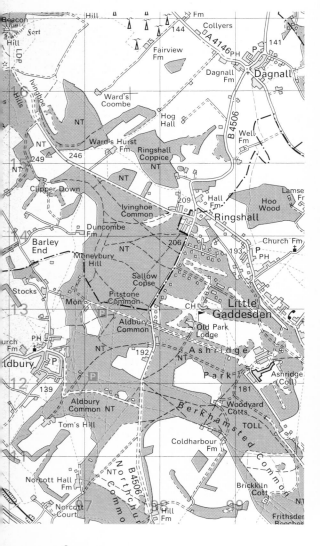

A birch thicket at the margin of an oakwood on Berkhamsted Common, Ashridge

BEECH LEAVES

The downy fringe is soon lost, with the thin shells of the bud, the leaf turning darker, tough, later persistent – better than straw for ladies' mattresses, claimed John Evelyn. This simplest leaf yet makes the tall *Fagus sylvatica* sovereign, able to shade out all opposition. Minute sensitivities also allow early sprays to leaf deep in the forest – the air still enough for a snapshot.

holidays avoid the roads by Ivinghoe Beacon: visit Ashridge at its best on a May morning, for opening beech leaves and new cherry blossom.

Wendover Woods *890 090 and 890 100, ♀ (♠), 400 acres plus 4 forest trails, FC*
You may feel as I do a twinge of regret that 400-odd acres of beechwoods were clear-felled for these conifers, but it should not be allowed to spoil one's appreciation, for these ridges and steep valleys clothed in firs and spruces provide a scenery just as appropriate to Britain, if you can imagine it before the Ice Age. Of course, these are not the varying ages and the probably impenetrable litter of dead trunks which would be characteristic of wild woodland, and you will not meet any wolf packs.

   Dancer's End, a nature reserve, *903 097*, 70 acres of typical Chiltern woodland, adjoins the north-east arm of Wendover Woods. Look for wood vetch, herb Paris, Solomon's seal, orchids and the Chiltern gentian.

Wendover Woods

Coombe Hill *847 072, NT*
Ellesborough Warren, Great Kimble
and **Pulpit Hill** *828 048,* ♀, *4m, easy*
or very difficult walking according to your
divergences from the footpath, NRs
This is a line of steep scarp slopes and ridge
paths looking over the Aylesbury Vale, and
traversing a great variety of scrubland backed
by fine beechwoods. Starting from the south-
west end, Pulpit Hill has a large area of
dogwood, impressively pink even in midwinter, fading off to scattered juniper bushes.
Above Great Kimble is a steep meadow
interestingly neglected and returning slowly to
forest via dog rose, field maple and sycamore.
Above this is a warren containing dogwood,
buckthorn, spindle, privet and an apparently
spontaneous small wood of English elm (a rare
occurrence), now completely dead. Beyond, in
a deep coombe with ungrassed chalk sides is a
natural history gem: a box coppice gone wild –
if it was not wild before it was coppiced.
Several walnuts are also to be found and these
have clearly regenerated naturally in the past,

though no seedlings are now present and the
trees die comparatively young. Spindle trees
survive the nibbling of rabbits. There are
patches of dogwood completely overlaid with
old man's beard. Amongst the box, which
ranges from low scrub to quite mature but
many-stemmed trees, are the stalks of *Daphne
laureola*, the spurge laurel. There are other
native trees, including a wych elm, long surviving the disease. But a group of Scots pines
on the hilltop is so nicely placed that one
suspects the perfecting touches of an
Edwardian lady, perhaps from nearby
Chequers. (You will be watched, probably, by
a very quiet man amongst the beeches.)

Boxwood was used on an industrial scale for
engraving illustrations between 1840 and 1880,
and these box trees probably owe their survival
to the printers of Aylesbury. A very dense
patch of woodland only to be described as
jungle keeps the north winds from this valley,
which must be prone to frost.

Through a natural arch of box on the east
side you pass to open grassland falling away to

Box trees at Great Kimble

escarpment woodland where a probably Iron Age earthwork known as Cymbeline's Castle supports wayward beeches. A stile leads to Ellesborough. Coombe Hill, beyond, belongs to the National Trust and is also ecologically interesting. The other sites are under the control of the County Naturalists' Trust. Please do not take or trample any living plants.

Woburn Park, *960 330*, has over 4 square miles of parkland with fine old oaks, cedars, and a hundred deer of at least nine different species.

There is a perfect spire of a 1930s vintage Leyland cypress behind the fairground. The Woburn Pinetum was famous about 1820 (when all conifers were *Pinus*). Now The Evergreens, a large belt of woodland at the north-west of the park, it is not one of the popular attractions of Woburn, but permission to explore it may be had in advance from the Forester. (Estate Office, Woburn Park, Beds, or ring 0525 25666.)

The ultimate in woodland walks must be to view great trees from a cable car, but to board one of these you have to enter The Animal Kingdom for £5; it might be worth a visit if you can park the family with the animals.

Bow Brickhill, *910 340*, offers the freedom of younger, more practical softwoods and,

In Woburn Park

from the steep, sandy outcrop of Aspley Heath, views over Milton Keynes.

Stockgrove Country Park, Heath and Reach *920 295*, ♀ *(♣)*, *LA*

This small woodland (600 yards long at the most) on sand with clay-with-flints started off with waymarked nature trails but is now riddled with paths – a little over-used I fear. Oak, most of it old coppice and now a cheerful open-textured wood (some small-leaved lime), merges nicely with patches of pine on the sands. There are some old pines and English cherry by the lake, which is a square-sided tank, probably deep. Bakers Wood, which is fenced off to the south-east, is planted with hemlock and cypress, still young.

A coppice of small-leaved lime in all its

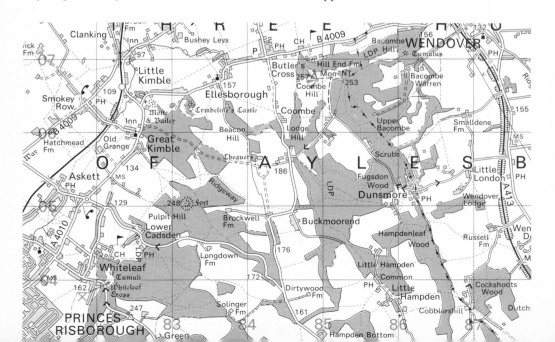

Ancient rowan in Stockgrove Country Park

splendour is down a muddy lane on the opposite side of the road – King's Wood. The land is private but bridleways are accessible and you can also walk from the north side. Somebody *drove* in with a load of waste paper.

WHITTLEWOOD FOREST

Bucknell Wood *660 451, about 450 acres, 2m or 1m, can be wet, FC*
This forestry plantation is to the north-west of Whittlewood Forest. The village of Silverstone is impossible to miss on the A43(T), and the road to the forest heads north to Abthorpe out of the village. With battery-hen production to the north and south, the wood may strike you as too rigidly productive in style, but the picnic place is open and attractive and the longer of the two walks takes in hardwoods as well as conifers. Once again, one must be grateful to the Forestry Commission for providing access to any woodland in an area of woods that are not easy to enter.

Bucknell Wood is actually in Northampton-

shire. For a look at the true beauty of North Buckinghamshire drive out of Silverstone in the opposite direction – towards Whittlebury – and turn right onto the A413 going south through the park. Here old, rugged oaks stand in true parkland style, but instead of roving deer or cattle there are root crops. Turn first left, still in the park. Here is a straight, quiet road which could provide a walk if you do not mind tarmac. The woods are private and not really walkable in, but the park oaks are magnificent – and I did try to photograph a muntjak without leaving the road, so it can't be bad.

Follow this road over slightly rising old forest land as it turns south-east towards Deanshanger, then turn sharp right on 'Gated Road' to Lillingstone Lovell. It is not really gated. Here you can walk in **Wicken Wood**, *731 413*, an old wood converted to conifers. Or you can rejoin the A413 and travel a mile south to look at Lillingstone Dayrell; just a minute church containing a magnificent pair of Dayrells; beside the church a house and a few trees. Every Englishman or woman has some favourite corner to recall England, if expatriated: this is mine. Alternatively fork left for Leckhampstead, a pretty place with a neat, simple church in a fold of the small hills.

Stowe Park, *670 370*, to the south of Silverstone, offers walking country in open parkland and you can stop practically anywhere on the wide verges of the approach roads, once under tall elm avenues, now replanted.

North of Newport-Pagnell **Gayhurst Wood**, called Buntsy Wood locally, *839 470*, has a bridleway through it. Turn off the B526 at Gayhurst, towards Hanslope. Half is old woodland, oak with rowan and other natives, and half young Corsican pine, suitably fenced off. There is a great variety of wet-loving trees and shrubs, and this is a lovely wild place, very rough walking – but not much of it before you hit the M1 to the south.

Stokepark Wood, *829 488*, near Stoke Goldington may be worth exploring: it also belongs to the Forestry Commission.

SOUTH OF HERTFORD

Great Wood *282 040*, ♀, *CP, about 500 acres, woodland trails mapped and waymarked, LA*
Closed at sunset and otherwise very well organized, this Country Park has much woodland lore to offer, with Bluebell Walk, The Beeches, Grimes Brook, Ash Grove, a coppice, a line of pollard hornbeams and a blackthorn copse. All is carefully conserved and observed. There is a charge for parking.

By wandering Hertfordshire lanes, or on foot north-east, if you are clever at footpaths, via a corner of Cheshunt Common, you will find Derry's Wood, joined to Wormley Wood, joined to Bencroft Wood.

Bencroft Wood and **Wormley Wood**
326 065, 332 065, ♀, *CC and WT*
Bencroft Wood contains a short woodland trail and also provides access to Wormley Wood, a 340-acre recent acquisition of the Woodland Trust. Oak/hornbeam with a long history of coppicing, this is the largest woodland of its type still in its 'semi-natural' state and is designated a grade 1 Site of Special Scientific Interest for this reason alone.

Carex pendula, with splendid construction in its triangular stem and great leaves stiffened by a double groove, spreads around a pond near the western car park. This drooping sedge is supposed to be common (in damp shade on heavy soils) in southern England, but here you can't miss it. It is the flower spikes, 6 inches

The hornbeams of Wormley Wood, now in the care of the Woodland Trust

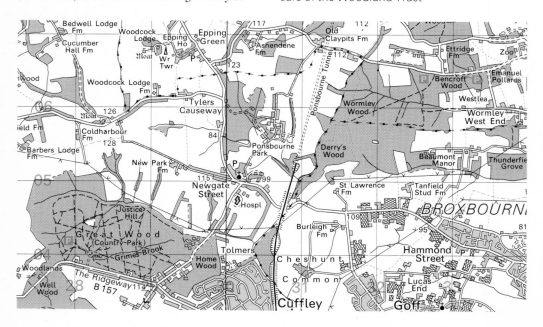

long on 6-foot-tall stems, which are pendulous. The hornbeams of Wormley Wood are a sight to be seen. They will be found along a well-marked track. Part of the wood was coniferized in the late 1970s and the Trust will restore it to hardwoods.

Galleyhill Wood 395 030, ♀, *about 100 acres, less than 1m long, an easy path, probably GLC*

This remote-seeming corner of Essex woodland is an outlier of Epping Forest. From the eastern end of the short bypass at the

northern side of Waltham Abbey take the road to Upshire, turning left after $\frac{1}{4}$ mile to Aimes Green. You can walk northwards by a dark hornbeam coppice into a serene old wood which actually looks like a forest, with great spreading oaks; the twisted, rather under-nourished hornbeams here behaving like underwood. The path runs by the east margin of the wood and you can look out over the fields, eventually emerging into them, the forest seeming to run out of trees. A few oaks standing isolated in long grass invite you to sit and reflect. If you did not know it, you would

The edge of the forest, Galleyhill Wood

Oak and hornbeam woodland, Galleyhill Wood

never believe you were only 12 miles from the City of London.

Hatfield House 236 085, *a stroll in the grounds of a great private house*
No one cannot want to see the house (1611) I guess, but once you have, the part of the garden open to visitors and the trees beyond it are something between a woodland garden and a small arboretum. What you can well believe is a real Jacobean pleached lime walk leads to a venerable chestnut leaning on sticks, and one

or two false acacias, *Robinia pseudoacacia*, that must be as old as any in the country. These stand among fine, large oaks which guard the west side of the house, with its curiously appealing squared-up and turreted architecture.

You can walk exactly southwards in a lime avenue (ordinary hybrid lime), then turn right into a plantation of tall specimen trees including a many-stemmed redwood and a gracious-looking beech. The entrance to the house and grounds is to the east of the A1000,

conurbations like Luton and Stevenage can seem to alter. Long may it remain so. I have done a few walks in these small woods, and have seen much of interest as well as getting stung and scratched. Let us leave a few · Hertfordshire secrets to be discovered by chance.

NORTH OF LUTON

Rowney Warren Wood *123 404,* ♠ ♀, *1½m, easy, FC*

The picnic place is nice, signposted RAF Chicksands on the A600, 2 miles north-west of Shefford. The forest walk or Robert Bloomfield Trail is a fairly simple affair – the wood is narrow and you can usually see the light at one side or the other. Pines Austrian and Corsican, larch, Douglas fir, and oak, birch and beech grow on little hills and dales of sand varying from a yellowish to dark reddish colour.

Oak trees round about on low wood-banks are stout-trunked, burred stragglers from another period: in the wood they are straight and narrow; the same species, you would hardly guess.

Chicksands Wood to the west is walkable through by a straight road from Appley Corner, *106 411*, if you like straight walks.

Maulden Wood on the A6 just north of Clophill has a picnic place away from the foul lay-by where you have to park, *072 395*. I suppose it's all right inside: there is a school trail, and a forest walk of 1½ miles, described by the Forestry Commission as pleasant – rather faint praise.

The Lodge, Sandy *188 478,* ♀ (♠), *100 acres, RSPB*

This wooded rise on greensand, 2 miles from the small town of Sandy, contains the headquarters of the RSPB. Parking is expensive just for a walk, but birdlife can be promised. The entrance is off the B1042 to Cambridge; you could always park outside and walk in. The whole wood is a bird sanctuary, open all year except 2 June, but to members only on Sundays and bank holidays.

Hatfield to Potters Bar road, in Old Hatfield. The park north of the house contains many ancient oaks scattered about in the traditional way of English parkland.

Hertfordshire is the most intricate and secretive of counties, broken into innumerable small valleys and corners – with many small woods. The Greens, Ends, Bottoms, Hills and Hoos, Commons, Streets and Burys are linked by an unbelievably intricate network of lanes that not even the presence nearby of

36	37	38
21	**22**	
18	19	

SOUTH-EAST ENGLAND
Essex and South Suffolk

Landranger sheets 167, 168, 169

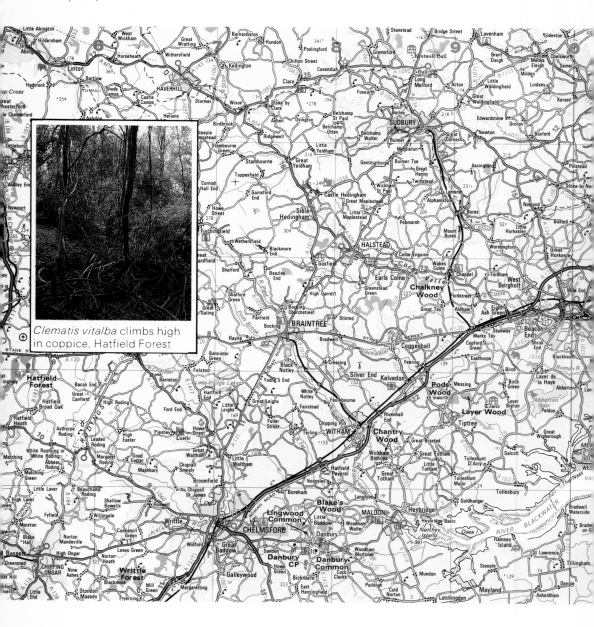

Clematis vitalba climbs high in coppice, Hatfield Forest

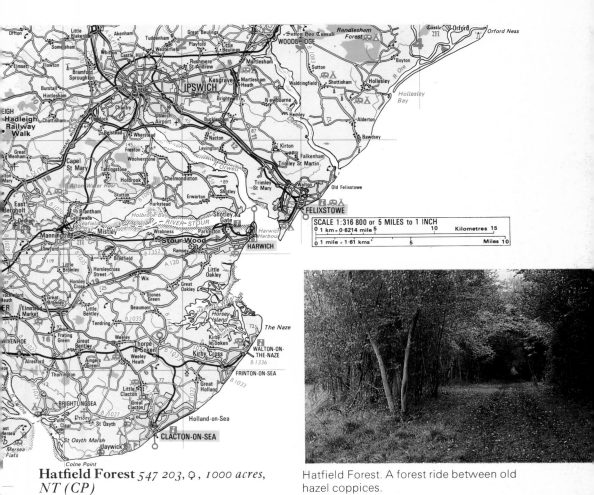

SCALE 1:316 800 or 5 MILES to 1 INCH

0 1 km = 0·6214 mile 5   10   Kilometres 15

0 1 mile = 1·61 kms   5   Miles 10

Hatfield Forest *547 203, ♀, 1000 acres, NT (CP)*

This important forest (not to be confused with Hatfield, Herts) is now indicated on the Ordnance Survey map as a Country Park, but it has been in the hands of the National Trust since 1924. At that time it was, largely, saved from the timber merchants by a far-sighted, quick-thinking – and rich – man, E. N. Buxton. Probably because since the Norman invasion it has been a royal hunting demesne, with its own special laws to protect the game, it has retained its ancient character through many generations of landowners. Notable amongst these were the

Hatfield Forest. A forest ride between old hazel coppices.

Houblons, who shared its manorial rights from 1729 onwards, and in 1854 bought out their neighbours the Barringtons of Old Barrington Hall. A Houblon made the lake, and another enclosed the land and then made drains which saved the forest from becoming a mire every winter. One Laetitia Houblon had complained of 'splashings in our forest', and perhaps it was she who planted the horse-chestnuts, at least one of which is remarkable for its unusual age and grandeur.

Although it is at the edge of the Great Essex Forest of old, this is not now the place to see ancient oaks. There were many, but they were felled in the early part of this century. Some very spectacular hybrid elms remained – with great buttresses and heavy horizontal limbs – but elm disease has killed them. The oldest trees, and most notable, are the great pollarded hornbeams just scattered about the open chases.

Hatfield Forest is unlike other scheduled Country Parks in that cars can park anywhere. For those unable to leave their vehicle, there is an area of old coppice and standards with all the richness of old woodland, which can be viewed from the metalled road. This 'safari' approach does not disturb birds such as tree creepers: walking does. Hanging lianas of traveller's joy, *Clematis vitalba*, are a particular feature of the coppices.

It is the coppices, now overgrown, which constitute the chief value of Hatfield to the student of woodland. Sadly, they are no longer cut as they were for centuries, on an eighteen-year rotation; for the first seven or so years of this period cattle were fenced out so that new shoots could become established – and along with them many wild flowers, including the oxlip for which the area is known. Beside grazing and pannage (pig food), commoners of the forest could take fuel and fencing material, so that the coppices would have always been tidy. Now, many of the woodland floors are permanently bare in the heavy shade.

Trees in the coppices are hazel, oak, wych elm and other elms, maple, birch and, darkest and dampest, hawthorn. The presence of large, old stools of wych elm and hornbeam within, for example, a hazel coppice says much for the historical nature of the forest: such trees would be 'self-sown' centuries ago. All the coppices have names, often those of the men who spent their lifetimes in the woods: Emblem's Coppice, Hampton's, Collin's Coppice. Wide, grassy rides, also named, ran between the cants and quiet visitors will certainly see fallow deer.

The soil is London clay over chalk but there is a sandy patch near the lake.

The excellent booklet, published by the National Trust and written by Anthony Buxton, includes a warning:

> The final result is a gradual transition from a large and balanced community of animal and plant life, unique in this part of Britain in its richness and variety of species, to a drab and homogeneous mixture of grasses and trees with only the commoner birds and insects.

At present, the forest serves many interests: there is a special section set aside as a nature reserve but car parking and all forms of relaxation, picnicking, ball games, dog walking, etc, continue in the forest; fox hunting is maintained because the Essex and Puckeridge Hunt has permanent rights; there is a nature trail which starts at the Shell House. Unfortunately some summer-visiting birds no longer appear in great numbers; whitethroats, blackcaps and sedge warblers are fewer, and the nightingale rarely sings; but teal visit the lake, and willow tit, hawfinch, woodcock, and water rail and snipe (one or two pairs) are known to breed.

Oak promoted from old coppice in a Writtle Forest wood

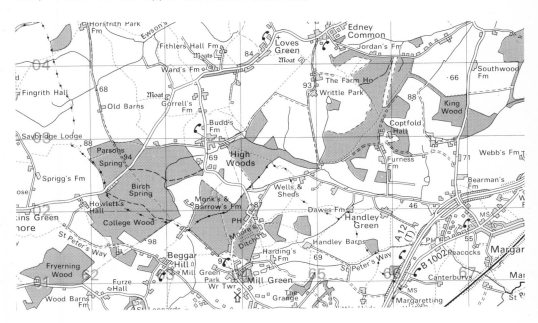

Writtle Forest is a vague area about 4 miles south-west of Chelmsford. I could find no formal access to woodland apart from many signposted footpaths in the area.

The Viper pub, *640 018*, has a small parking space opposite with a footpath sign to Handley Barns. That particular footpath, number 20, is not very well wooded. A mile down the road towards High Woods village a path is signposted into the woods south-west of the road, that is, on your left. This wood appears to have no name. It is oak, with chestnut, birch and hornbeam, and there is a steep bank and ditch in the middle. The wood is not perhaps special, but it is very quiet and easy to walk in. Turn left on emerging – which may be on to the farm road or the motor road to Mill Green. On the other side of the road is a birchwood surrounding Moore's Ditch. You may then meet a footpath returning to the Viper. You will walk 2 or 3 miles according to the route you take through the wood.

The footpaths are very well signposted in this area if they are not always clear on the ground, and most woodland paths appear to be open to serious walkers. But this is a forest only in name, like many another.

On the east side of Chelmsford, the village of Danbury is a centre of great interest for its woods and commons. Danbury is on high ground – 300 feet above sea-level is high for Essex. For this reason alone the area has a long history, at least back to the Anglo-Saxons. The common was used as an army camp in the Napoleonic Wars, and there are some remains of this occupation, but less of the modern army exercises which also took place here. Smugglers, with goods imported to the Blackwater Estuary, are said to have grazed their horses on the common, waiting for nightfall. Today, the village still feels like a village even though it has a bank and a large population in the many secluded houses fronting its narrow lanes.

Danbury Country Park *770 048*, ♀, *41 acres*

This park has parking for 200 cars and is visited by 60,000 people a year, and their dogs.

The picnic area would accommodate 5000, and there are lakes for catching small fishes. A long triangle of plantation surrounds some great, sculptured trunks of oak, much, much older than the rest of the wood; some are twisted and scarred, seemingly eloquent in death. Others still support leafy wandering limbs. All were last pollarded in Good King Charles' time. There are hornbeams and beeches too.

A notice-board complains of erosion caused by many feet, and sensibly suggests we go somewhere else next time. However, if you want to see these histrionic wooden torsos, take the Chelmsford road out of Danbury for ½ mile and turn left into Wood Hill Road.

Danbury Common *782 045*, ♀, *many paths, NT*

It is just south of Danbury church and fans out from the parking place in a pattern of open and

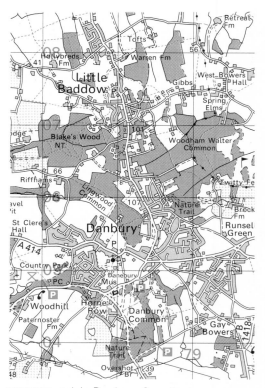

OPPOSITE: oak in Danbury Country Park

wooded land. In a way it is ordinary; patches of gorse and birch with odd small oaks and sallows, and in between bracken and grass, and also some reedy stretches. But it is lovely, there is no denying it. One can see why the National Trust took it over, and why everyone wanted to come and live here, and why it is criss-crossed with so many little paths. There is hornbeam coppice – that sounds so work-manlike, and yet it is a fairyland, even in a cold drizzle. Old oaks grow on the boundary and two-seeded hawthorn on the higher ground.

Lingwood Common *784 057, ♀, steep and muddy, NT*

On the other side of the Chelmsford road (which is very busy), Lingwood is densely wooded, and completely hemmed in by suburban-style houses. It is dark and steep, and there are more chestnuts and oaks than on

Danbury Common. There are the expected hornbeams, some, on the well-marked boundary bank, reminiscent of Arthur Rackham's fairyland illustrations. On the top of the hill to the east side is a patch of oak coppice; unusual in Essex. The open field which occupies the south-western part is reverting to scrub, and it would be a good idea if some of the local riders grazed their horses here.

Blake's Wood, *775 068*, is also National Trust property, 80 acres of hornbeam and chestnut coppice near Little Baddow, 2 miles to the north-west of Danbury.

At Tiptree, beyond Maldon, another, larger stretch of preserved heathland is much less organized: the wide, open Tiptree Heath is south of the B1022 to Maldon. On the same road out of Tiptree to Colchester stands **Pods Wood**, *892 175*. Like **Layer Wood**, *913 175*, beyond, it has been efficiently coniferized, but the trees are younger than at Layer Wood and the sawyers are not yet at work. There are wide rides, as you might expect, and a very few native trees by their edges. At the Tiptree side of Pods Wood there remains a long strip of bony, coppiced hornbeam which was probably left as shelter for the seedling pines. The path is easy – it seems to be used mostly by children. This belt of old coppice, so full of its own character compared with the equally functional pines, gives a good idea of what the woods must have been like when everyday life depended on their produce. The pinewoods are remote from our lives, only supplying a pathetic fraction of the national demand for softwood, and supporting a much-reduced wildlife. There is no formal access and there is nowhere in particular to park your car.

Wickham Bishops' **Chantry Wood**, *838 130*, is also an overgrown hornbeam coppice – very attractive but only partly open to walkers, who are probably mostly local. Old hornbeam coppices are almost collectors' items in south Essex, a sort of bygone woodland, useful for walking your dog in. Chantry Wood is indicated by a notice. It is on a narrow road between Witham and Wickham.

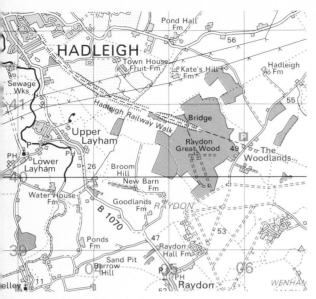

Hadleigh Railway Walk

Hadleigh Railway Walk *055 405 (The Woodlands old station)*, ♀, *2m, easy walking*
Raydon Great Wood, ½ mile south-east of Hadleigh, Suffolk, has no access apart from the Hadleigh Railway Walk. The wood is under private forestry, well guarded at the sides but penetrated by the old single-track railway which has been most imaginatively converted. You can cover the 2 miles of straight track from Hadleigh, through orchards and scrub to The Woodlands, Raydon, under your own steam. Both the wood and the railway banks are rather overgrown, limiting the light for flowers, among which are orchids. The north side of the wood is fairly original oakwood, the south much planted.

Cotoneaster microphylla, a garden plant, grows at the western edge facing an old airfield.

Chalkney Wood *871 275*, ♀, *200 acres, 63 accessible, easy muddy routes, CC*
This important wood is 1 mile south-east of Earls Colne: take the Great Tey road which turns off between the Bulldog Garage and the George Inn. Roadside parking for several cars is available but there is no attempt at institutionalization.

This is a mediaeval wood. Boundaries shown as well established on a map of 1598 remain today. The north-eastern two-thirds were coniferized in the 1950s, not so thoroughly as to destroy all evidence of the former tree population. Small-leaved lime in the south-western third is now coppiced, some remaining elegantly overgrown as a background to oak and ash standards. This is the best place to see small-leaved lime coppice.

A straight, wide path divides the wood, and a hollow-way identified as an early British road adopted by the Romans intersects this at a shallow angle. There are numerous ancient pits and hollows.

The complex of long-established woodland patterns here is worthy of detailed study, with Rackham (1980) as the infallible guide. He points to ash/hazel with maple on calcareous patches (at the south corner particularly); to areas where chestnut is co-dominant with lime; to groups of aspen, more or less evenly scattered, and alder at the rather inaccessible

Part of the varied pattern of coppice and standards in Chalkney Wood

northern side, by streams, but also in small amounts near the south on a plateau. He has analysed the original vegetation of the coniferized portion, and shows that the lime area interpenetrated with a hornbeam-dominated northern section. There was some elm in the small valleys, and a different elm, used to hedge the boundaries, has crept into the wood, but only shallowly. He does not mention some sallow, but he identifies two stools of wild service.

Some lime stools in the middle of the south-western – original – part are at least 5 feet across, rotten but still putting out shoots. Paths or tracks in the coppice wander in a serpentine way amongst the stools in what is described as a mediaeval system – partly replaced by straight rides. When the lime was cut recently, after a lapse of more than fifty years in the coppicing cycle, raspberry, dormant in the soil, suddenly became prolific. Bluebell dominates the field layer, but there are also primroses, bracken and bramble: dog's mercury in the ash-maple-hazel areas.

The dark earth of the fields from here to Coggeshall has probably been under the plough for as long as the woods have been cut. This is a clean, shapely countryside with old, black wooden barns and well-kept, handsome houses. Hedges now are few, and the landscape is returning to a pattern suggesting the open fields of long ago.

Stour Wood, *190 315*, Wrabness, is an important acquisition of the Woodland Trust in a part of the country where woodland is very scarce. It is a chestnut coppice, but a more diverse distribution of trees is to be encouraged in the future – there are eighteen species of tree already, including the wild service tree, which alone indicates that this is an ancient woodland. From the B1352 to Ramsey, there are two footpaths, one roughly at each end of the wood. The Stour Estuary is just to the north and the wood is managed by the Royal Society for the Protection of Birds as part of an internationally important reserve.

Index